30 Days
to a More Incredible
Marriage

from *Today's Christian Woman* magazine

Edited by
RAMONA CRAMER TUCKER

Tyndale House Publishers, Inc.
WHEATON, ILLINOIS

Library of Congress Cataloging-in-Publication Data

30 days to a more incredible marriage / edited by Ramona Cramer Tucker.
    p.   cm.
   "TCW books from Today's Christian woman magazine."
   ISBN 0-8423-0591-2 (sc)
   1. Christian women—Prayer-books and devotions—English. 2. Wives—Prayer-books and devotions—English. 3. Marriage—Religious aspects—Christianity. I. Tucker, Ramona Cramer.
BV4844.A12   1998
242'.6435—dc21   98-23843

Printed in the United States of America

03 02 01 00 99 98
10 9 8 7 6 5 4 3 2

CONTENTS

INTRODUCTION

$\mathcal{D}$o you wish that

- your husband could read your mind—and you could read his?
- you'd known more about marriage . . . before you said, "I do"?
- you and your husband were closer emotionally?
- you and your spouse handled money differently?
- you knew how to deal with the times your man drives you nuts?
- you'd married someone else?
- you and your husband had more friends?
- you were more creative in making your guy feel special?

Marital questions—we all have them. And the ones above are just for starters. We also wonder how to deal with times of disagreement, how to handle opposite personalities with celebration instead of frustration, how to decode one another's sounds and sighs. If children arrive, we may wonder whether or not we'll ever have sex again. We throw up our hands as we discover a job is changing again, meaning another move. We question God when our faith is growing and our spouse's doesn't seem to be.

This book provides perspective for a wide range of marriage questions, including, "What if my spouse and I are spiritually mismatched?" "Who should mind the money?" "How can I show my man I cherish him—every day?" and "What should I do if I've fallen out of love with my husband?"

Each day provides a Scripture passage, a story or message, a quote from a person such as Susan Ashton, Elisa Morgan, or CeCe Winans, and reflections on a topic, as well as "A Step Further" to help you grow in a particular area of your marriage. In addition, the "Faith Focus" will help you evaluate how you and your spouse are currently doing and where you'd like to be and will provide ideas on how to get there. The "Prayer Pointer" will assist you in focusing your prayers on the topic for the day.

In just thirty short days, this book will give you handholds that can transform your marriage—enriching your communication, intimacy, and spiritual walk together. As Scripture says, "Our lives are a fragrance presented by Christ to God" (2 Cor. 2:15). So let's spread the aroma of Christ around—particularly in our marriage—for his glory!

Ramona Cramer Tucker
Editor
Today's Christian Woman magazine

As the Scriptures say, "A man leaves his father and mother and is joined to his wife, and the two are united into one." This is a great mystery, but it is an illustration of the way Christ and the church are one.

Ephesians 5:31-32

*W*hen my husband, Jeff, and I first met, we were radically different. I enjoyed ballet and theater; he liked action-packed movies. I preferred to sew and cook; he liked to work on computers and cars.

But over the past twelve years of marriage, we've discovered the joy of Ephesians 5:31-32: how two very different personalities can work together in harmony *because* of our different gifts.

If you and your husband are poles apart in personality, likes, and dislikes, here's how you can reconcile those differences—and have fun doing it!

Reconcilable Differences

During the past twenty-three years, my husband, Mark, and I have tripped over many truths about life—and sidestepped a few more. Kind of like Dick Van Dyke and his pesky ottoman.

We had a lot going against us back in 1975. We were twenty years old with two years of college remaining, and we had never lived on our own. We came from different backgrounds. Mark grew up on meat and potatoes, while I was used to hamburger-surprise casserole. He preferred water-skiing on a steamy lake over my hiking in the cool mountains. But we had two key things in our favor: determination and our Christian faith. We were committed to each other and to our growing relationship with God.

Yet just because we were both determined to make our marriage work didn't mean I didn't want to grab Mark in a headlock a few times. (And vice versa.)

When we were first married, we thought it was necessary to like the same things. So with innocent accommodation, I tried pan-fried chicken and Mark tried chicken à la king. I tried to watch basketball, and he tried to watch black-and-white movies. But once we stopped trying so hard to blend our individual tastes into one, we learned there are advantages to not liking the same things. I never have to worry about Mark's snarfing up my rhubarb pie, and he never has to worry about my taking a bite of his pumpkin.

Through appreciating our differences, our horizons have been broadened. Because of me, Mark's experienced the excitement of live theater. And because of him, I've learned to sing "Take Me out to the Ball Game" during the seventh-inning stretch.

We've discovered that our differences don't diminish our life together—they enhance it. Now, instead of highlighting our differences, we work together to make things fair and equal. For instance, we often "make deals":

"I'll clean the kitchen if you'll vacuum."

"I'll take the kids to the movie if you'll pick them up."

And when one of us decides to go beyond "the deal" and do more than what's agreed on, we experience the joy of fulfilling what Romans 12:10 says: "Love each other with genuine affection, and take delight in honoring each other."

Good marriages—those that satisfy and last—require time, attention, and nurturing.

DR. BARBARA CHESSER

Mark and I also remember that we didn't choose our parents, our siblings, our aunts and uncles. And our kids didn't choose us. The only kin I've ever chosen was Mark. And he chose me. Our parents will pass away. Our precious children will grow up and move on. But Mark and I are in it for life. So Mark and I have an ever-after philosophy. We believe our marriage vows are not traditional hokum, that the ceremony has endured for so long because its words are lasting: "For better or worse, for richer or poorer, in sickness and in health, to love and to cherish till death us do part."

I do. We do. And with the Lord's help, that takes us a long way toward keeping our commitment—even when differences crop up. *Nancy Moser*

A Step Further

Five Ways to Reconcile Differences

1. *Don't sweat the small stuff.* Remember
   God's wise words in Ephesians 4:2: "Be
   patient with each other," and allow each
   other unimportant foibles.
2. *Turn "me" thoughts into "us" thoughts.*
   Instead of working to win an argument,
   think about how you can serve God and
   your spouse.
3. *Consider the consequences.* Just because
   you *think* something doesn't mean it
   should pop out of your mouth.
4. *Balance each other.* Uplift each other in
   difficult times. Bring common sense to
   relational issues and financial purchases.
5. *Dream, plan, and pray.* Half the fun of
   any goal is not only getting there but
   talking about it too. God waits for you
   to consult him (Prov. 16:9). Three heads
   are definitely better than one!   *NM*

Faith Focus

In what ways are you and your spouse different? How could those differences actually work for your good as a family unit? Do you have a "today only" philosophy or an "ever after" philosophy? What steps do you need to take to reconcile your differences?

Prayer Pointer

Thank God for the life partner he's given you. Ask him to help you see your differences as positive gifts given by a gracious God. Pray that you'll be patient in the process of marriage as you work together with your spouse to glorify God.

LET EVERYTHING YOU SAY BE
GOOD AND HELPFUL, SO THAT
YOUR WORDS WILL BE AN EN-
COURAGEMENT TO THOSE WHO
HEAR THEM.

 EPHESIANS 4:29

*I*f someone were to step into your household on a Sunday morning before church, what would she hear? Pleasant, edifying conversation—or something else? If you're in the "something else" category, you're not alone. Statistics show that the times Christian families struggle the most with their words and attitudes are before and after church.

An old adage says, "Familiarity breeds contempt," but Scripture tells us that our words—whether spoken in private or public—should help instead of harm. If you want to change the tone of your marriage so that you treat your spouse at home the way you do in front of others, here's help.

How Does Your Marriage Sound?

"Stupid!" I exclaimed.

Water splashed the counter and spilled over to our kitchen floor as my husband, Jack, and I grabbed towels to mop it up. Jack, not realizing I'd already made coffee the night before in our new, opaque-drip coffeepot, had poured another pot of water into the already full container.

The split second after my one-word epithet came out, I wanted to stuff it right back into my mouth. But it was too late.

Most of us don't deliberately set out to speak derogatorily to our spouse. Yet somehow, over the years, habits develop, and the sound of our marriage may sometimes become discordant.

If only each and every one of us would filter all we say through Ephesians 4:29, "Let everything you say be good and helpful, so that your words will be an encouragement to those who hear them." If I were paraphrasing this verse, it would come out something like this: "Don't let a single hurtful word come out of your mouth, but only speak what is helpful, encouraging, kind, beneficial, and loving. May your jokes be at your own expense and not at others'. Give your spouse frequent verbal pats on his shoulder, ones that build him up. Don't retaliate if he gets a dig in, but turn it around and make a kind and loving remark."

Years ago, Jack and I had the opportunity to observe a family whose sarcasm had graduated from funny to downright lethal. Then the Lord got hold of the wife's heart. She confessed her unkindness—her failure to edify her family, her lack of tongue control. She didn't talk to her family about her decision but simply determined, with God's help, to stop using sarcasm. The change soon became evident to her family, and they asked her about it. Quietly she told them the Lord had convicted her of saying unkind things. Soon it became a joy to be around the entire family.

Sound impossible? You bet! Impossible, that is, for us incredibly weak humans. Fortunately, God doesn't leave us without significant help: himself. He says, "Discretion will protect you, and understanding will guard you" (Prov. 2:11, NIV). Discretion is knowing when to speak and when to keep still.

> *No matter how difficult our situation,*
> *our attitude is our choice.*
> MARY WHELCHEL

God never gives us a command he doesn't give us his strength to obey—if we ask him. So his commands, such as "don't talk too much, for it fosters sin. Be sensible and turn off the flow!" (Prov. 10:19); "the godly speak words that are helpful" (10:32); "some people make cutting remarks, but the words of the wise bring healing" (12:18); and "those who control their tongue will have a long life; a quick retort can ruin everything" (13:3) are possible to obey.

If we're open to God and ask for his help, he can—and will—turn our marriage around for his glory and our joy.

Carole Mayhall

11

A STEP FURTHER

Sound Check for Harmony

1. *Identify negative habits.* Do you use sarcasm (humor at the expense of others) instead of loving honesty?
2. *Pray for God's help.* "The Lord grants wisdom! From his mouth come knowledge and understanding" (Prov. 2:6).
3. *Ask a close friend—one who knows both of you—this tough question:* "How would you describe the way my husband and I sound as we talk with each other?"
4. *Ask your husband:* "What changes in our communication would you appreciate most? What would you be willing to do to help me change?"
5. *Take the twenty-year view.* When tempted to correct your spouse in public, ask yourself, *Twenty years from now, will it make any difference to the listeners?* If not, keep your mouth shut.   CM

Faith Focus

How does your marriage sound? More specifically, how do you think you sound to your husband? Which of the following adjectives would he say describes your relationship: funny, gracious, sarcastic, considerate, irritable, critical, or appreciative? What "sound checks" does your marriage need to undergo to make it more God-honoring?

Prayer Pointer

Ask God to pinpoint which speech patterns or actions toward your spouse are unedifying. Then pray, asking God to forgive you—and to give you the courage to change, even if your spouse's behavior and words remain the same.

LOVE NEVER GIVES UP, NEVER
LOSES FAITH, IS ALWAYS HOPEFUL,
AND ENDURES THROUGH EVERY
CIRCUMSTANCE. LOVE WILL LAST
FOREVER.

1 CORINTHIANS 13:7-8

*A*h, those early dating days—filled with romance, surprise gifts, special dinners, and long hand-in-hand walks and talks. The time when you just *knew* God had given you your knight in shining armor—and you were his chosen lady!

Then you got married and discovered the many-faceted sides to each other's personality. For many couples, the first year or two become a test of the relationship. That's when the words of 1 Corinthians 12:7-8 can help: "Love never gives up."

Here's what one couple discovered about "I do" after they "did."

What I Didn't Know about "I Do" before I Did

Before my wife, Mary, and I exchanged our wedding vows forty years ago, our pastor gave us wise premarital counsel, and my dad took me aside and filled me with his accumulated wisdom. Even Buzz, the gas station attendant, offered some helpful hints about marriage. And my classmates who'd married a few years earlier were on hand for suggestions:

- "Always pick up your socks, and she'll love you in spite of your other faults."
- "Take the side of the bed farthest from the bathroom. She'll have to go more often than you."
- "Never go to bed angry, but don't let her get in the last word."
- "Share everything. If two people love each other, they can share anything."

Being a quick learner, I decided to live by those adages and assumed I knew everything I needed to know. But two days into our honeymoon, I realized it takes more than a few words to prepare couples for that eventful ride of their life: marriage.

It was that "share everything" idea that turned sour first. Taking this literally, I decided our honeymoon was the time to begin sharing as a way of showing love. So I didn't take any toothpaste. (Well, the real reason I didn't take it was . . . I forgot.) I knew we loved each other—we could share.

That's when I began to experience culture shock. Mary

used a brand totally alien to my required taste. And that was only the beginning! She also squeezed the tube from the middle! I discovered the hard way that no matter how much a husband and wife love each other, some things can't be shared—especially toothpaste.

When I publicly promised Mary on June 6, 1958, that I would love her, I thought I knew what I was talking about. Little did I know how much she and I would grow in love.

True love is expressed as much by what we do as by what we give.
REBECCA K. GROSENBACH

A few years ago, I had knee surgery. Nothing dramatic. They put me to sleep, poked three holes in my knee, scraped out what wasn't working, and sent me home. But my knee hurt, and I didn't recover well from the anesthesia. I threw up on the bed. Through the years, students and football players I coach have told me how important I was to them. Church people have expressed their love and care. But none of those folks showed up that night to help clean up the mess.

The only person who was there was that sweet young woman who took me for better or worse forty years ago and has been on the receiving end of both! All the premarital counseling we received could never have proved to me what I know now, without a shadow of a doubt: I wouldn't trade a moment of Mary's unconditional love for anything in this world. And I can't wait to see what lies around the bend for us on this wild and wonderful ride of marriage.
Cliff Schimmels

A STEP FURTHER

A Humorous Look at Personality Types

1. *Thrower vs. keeper.* If keepers married keepers, houses would be too full; if throwers married throwers, landfills would be used up.
2. *Gobbler vs. slow eater.* If engaged couples finish a meal more than four minutes apart, they should get extra counseling.
3. *Talker vs. silent type.* I learned it wasn't worth it to drive two hundred miles in silence because I was too stubborn to ask for directions. My wife learned not to get angry when I wasn't wise enough to figure out what she was upset about.
4. *Concrete vs. abstract speech.* For example, "Why don't you order dessert? I'd just like a couple bites" really means "I have a chocolate craving bigger than the Grand Canyon, but I'm too embarrassed to order in front of these people." CS

Faith Focus

What did you discover about "I do" after you "did"? In what ways have you and your spouse worked together through these surprises? Are there areas you still need to work on? If so, which ones?

Prayer Pointer

Thank God for his wisdom in bringing you just the spouse you need to help you grow spiritually and relationally. Ask him to guide you as you talk with your spouse and work through any marital surprises.

Serve each other in humility, for "God sets himself against the proud, but he shows favor to the humble." So humble yourselves under the mighty power of God, and in his good time he will honor you.

1 Peter 5:5-6

*H*ave you ever heard the saying "A man never knows what's in a woman's mind"? It's true—just ask any guy. (You can tell which ones to ask because they're the ones who look really confused!)

So why do we expect our spouse to just *know* when to be home for dinner—or when to plan a date night? And then when he doesn't meet our expectations, why are we disappointed or disgusted?

Scripture gives an antidote to heavy expectations: service in humility (1 Pet. 5). So the next time you wish your husband could read your mind, here's how to encourage him—without great expectations.

Great Expectations

It had been an especially difficult day. Tired and feeling sorry for myself, I decided that cooking dinner was too much work and that I'd like my husband, Jack, to take me out to eat. But I didn't want to have to ask! Instead, I envisioned exactly what would happen when Jack came home from work: He would take one look at my drooping shoulders and weary expression and ask, "What's the matter, honey? Had a hard day?"

Me, sighing, "Well, it hasn't been the best."

Him, giving me a hug, "Tell you what. Why don't we go out to eat and you can tell me all about it?"

However, when Jack did come home from work, the first thing he said to me was, "Hi, honey," and then he disappeared into the study to watch the evening news. To my disappointment, my scenario never played out the way I'd imagined it.

For those of us who face the dilemma of frequently expecting our husband to "read our mind," we may need to ask ourselves these questions:

Do I really know my husband—and myself? Many wives haven't made a deep enough study of their husband's personality to realize that it often isn't a matter of not wanting to fulfill our expectations—it's a matter of not understanding them. So take a personality test; ask questions of knowledgeable people; study spiritual gifts. Talk about the ways in which you and your husband respond differently.

Do I accept my husband's limitations? People who have studied the left-brain, right-brain theory tell us women may have more connectors between the two sides of the brain, making it easier for them to connect the logical, practical left side with the creative, verbal right side. If this theory is true, there may be a legitimate physiological reason why many men have difficulty tuning into a woman's needs. As a result, we may unfairly expect our husband to do what he may have trouble doing naturally.

Is pride hindering me from expressing my needs? Sometimes pride comes in the way of my saying to Jack, "You know, I need a hug right now. I'm feeling a bit lonely." But if we swallow that pride and humbly tell our spouse what we think, need, or feel—even if it sounds stupid or feels awkward—marital communication will improve.

> *Every day I choose how I will view whatever situation I find myself in. Will I be a victor or a victim? What gives God the glory?*
> GEORGIA COMFORT

Will humor help? I have a friend who tries to tell her husband what she needs in a lighthearted way. While her husband is present, she speaks for both of them, expressing what she wishes he would say.

So I tried it with Jack the night I really wanted to go out for dinner. Instead of expecting Jack to pick up on my tiredness, I said, "Jack, I had a hard day. I need you to ask me, 'Will going out for supper help?'"

And he said, "Will going out for supper help?"

"Yes," I said, and we both laughed. (And we did go out for supper, too!)   *Carole Mayhall*

A STEP FURTHER

Resolving Marital Expectations

1. *When your mind forms the thought*
   But he should know how I feel, *stop!*
   Instead of allowing yourself to become
   disappointed by your expectations, ask
   the Lord to help you communicate your
   needs openly, honestly, and clearly.
2. *Evaluate your own thoughts and feelings,
   needs and wants.* Unless *you* know what
   you want, how can you expect your
   husband to know?
3. *Be fair in your relationship.* Instead of
   mentally writing a script you expect
   your unsuspecting husband to follow,
   resolve to write it together. You'll be
   glad you did!

CM

Faith Focus

Do you expect your husband to read your mind—to know what you think and how you feel without your telling him? Which expectations do you think are realistic—and which aren't? How can you encourage better communication without great expectations?

Prayer Pointer

Thank God that he knows all things—even when your husband doesn't. Ask him to help you be realistic in your expectations. Pray for the Lord's help as you and your spouse learn more about "reading each other's mind."

As iron sharpens iron,

a friend sharpens a friend.

Proverbs 27:17

*I*t's Saturday morning, and a buddy phones your husband: "Hey, let's go out for breakfast!" What's your response? Do you

(a) fume—because it'll mess up your schedule for cleaning out the garage?

(b) smile—because you're glad your husband has a good friend?

"Male bonding" may look different from women's friendships (much of it takes place over activities such as barbecuing, fixing cars, putting a new roof on a house, attending a sports event). You may even consider it a waste of time. But if you long for the best in your spouse, encourage him to build the kind of friendship Proverbs 27:17 talks about. Here's why!

Is Your Husband a "Lone Ranger"?

"Have a good time!" my husband, Fritz, says, waving good-bye as my friend Barb and I head off to the women's meeting at church. We're set for a night of deep sharing and baked goods, while Fritz's big night will revolve around dragging out the garbage and making sure our daughter, Amanda, gets her homework done.

This type of scenario repeats itself over and over at our house. If the phone rings for me, it's likely to be a friend. If it's for him, it's probably somebody offering to clean our air ducts. I open my soul to a confidante; he jokes around with our friend Tom the handyman when Tom comes to fix something at our house.

Sometimes I wish Fritz had more friends, guys he could call up and say, "Hey, wanna go to the high school baseball game tomorrow?" I don't mean to imply that my spouse is socially comatose. He enjoys it when we have other couples over. And he has an admirable gift for making small talk with the hardworking businessmen he sees in the course of his workday. But when I hear about men who have prayer partners, men who open up to other men, I wish my husband would reach out this way. Why? I guess it's because I long for the best for my spouse, and that "best" includes the gift of friends who help us grow spiritually, who laugh with us and challenge us.

But Fritz may not be as lonely as I think. While most women tend to be relationally oriented, communicating their feelings easily and openly, men relate better around a shared task or recreation. What may look superficial to me—Fritz joshing with Tom as Tom works on our house—

may well help meet my husband's needs for male companionship.

I've realized I should avoid forcing my spouse to be someone he's not. Fritz and I know men who are involved in church, civic, and school activities, men who seem to know half the town. Doing all this seems like a great way to make friends, but it isn't for Fritz. "I just don't like doing 'group' kinds of things," he's admitted to me.

It's wise to pay attention to the clues my husband gives me. The other day, Fritz mentioned an acquaintance of his. "You know, I think Bill would like to be friends," he said. While I shouldn't read too much into this statement, it could mean Fritz is opening the door to friendship—and I can help that process by gently encouraging him to follow up.

Today's "men's movement" underscores the need men have for male friendships that goes beyond spending an afternoon at Home Depot. Sometimes men just need a man's perspective.

JAMES CHARIS

But sometimes staying out of the way is wise. Recently Fritz and I had dinner with a couple. After the meal, the guys sat at the table, talking over coffee, while my friend and I withdrew. Although I was interested in what they were discussing, I realized it was best to leave those two to their own devices—to give friendship a chance.

Elizabeth Cody Newenhuyse

A Step Further

Rustling Up Some Friends

1. *Create opportunities for friendship.* Planning a shared activity with other families or encouraging him to cultivate a hobby he can share with other men can create a climate where friendship can flourish.

2. *Gently guide your husband through relational waters.* Offer little hints on how to make small talk. On the way to a social event, suggest some conversation starters.

3. *Respect your spouse's need for occasional solitude.* If he doesn't feel like being Mr. Congeniality sometimes, accept and honor it. After all, you married *him*, not him and his buddies. And give your husband the freedom to pursue some of his interests—without you.

4. *Pray for your husband's needs.* Ask God to show him and you a way to help him connect with others—his way, not yours.

ECN

Faith Focus

Does your husband have many friends, few friends, or not really any close friends? How do you handle his contacts with friends—with jealousy, with frustration, or with joy? In what ways can you encourage your husband to form friendships with males who can encourage him relationally, emotionally, and spiritually?

Prayer Pointer

Thank God for your own friendships. Ask God to help you be willing to share your husband—for *his* good—even when household tasks need to be done. Pray for creative ways to encourage friendship in your husband's life without being pushy.

EARS TO HEAR AND EYES TO SEE—

BOTH ARE GIFTS FROM THE LORD.

PROVERBS 20:12

*D*uring our first year of marriage, my husband, Jeff, asked me to hand him a Phillips screwdriver as he worked on a car. "Oh, you mean the flower-head one?" I responded. Twelve years later, I *know* the proper name for it—and I can tell you about horsepower and rpm's, too!

It's been fun to see how our respective gifts have come in handy. For instance, Jeff knew exactly which sewing machine to buy me (lots of horsepower). We love Proverbs 20:12 because it encourages us to treat our differences as gifts rather than frustrations.

If your couple communication sometimes needs translating, here are some handy tips.

Can We Talk?

My wife, Elaine, and I were on our way home from a ten-day tour of Melbourne, Australia.

"What they really need is a male-female translation tape," Elaine announced as she pointed to the "Learn Swahili in Just Thirty Days" ad in the airline magazine. "Sometimes I have no idea where you're coming from."

"Huh?" I responded out of a jet-lag stupor. Then, eyeing her open bag of peanuts, I said, "Are you going to eat the rest of those?"

"See—that's what I mean," she said, moving as far away as anyone can in a twelve-inch-wide airplane seat. She was silent through the next two time zones.

Maybe she's right, I thought. *There are times when it feels as though men and women aren't even in the same communication cosmos!*

Since that Australian tour, Elaine and I have tried harder to become "bilingual" rather than try to change each other's dialect. Though not completely fluent, we're making progress. If you're puzzled sometimes about how to relate to a person of the opposite gender, consider the following clues to female/male communication:

Men tend to be literal; women tend to be figurative. We men are used to talking about 3/8-inch wrenches, 8 megabytes of RAM, 2,500 rpm's, and a score of 104-96 in the NBA play-offs—things you can see, measure, quantify. Male communication usually encompasses all the emotion of a computer manual. So when women use word pictures or superlatives such as "We never go out," men tend to respond literally: "What do you mean, we never go out? We went out to dinner and a movie a couple months ago!"

Men prefer "just the facts"; women tell the whole story. Realizing this, Elaine now switches into her "Barbara Walters" mode and asks, "So, how did you feel about it?" when she wants more detail. And she's learned to brief me with the who, what, when, where, and why before going on to what I consider "less important" details.

Men withdraw under stress; women prefer to vent. A male sitting on the couch with his nose in the newspaper might be silently shouting, *I've had a hard day, and I want to escape into the world of mayhem to console myself that my life isn't as bad as it is in Iraq!*

> ### Communication involves two parts: first, saying what you want to get across; second, saying it in a way the other person can receive it.
> DR. DIANE MANDT LANGBERG

Now when I'm in a vegetative state, Elaine simply says, "You look like something's bothering you. Let me know when you want to talk about it." Then she does her own thing until I feel like verbalizing.

When Elaine shares a problem, I try to give her my full attention and fight the urge to provide an immediate answer. Sometimes all she wants is for me to listen and say, "I understand."

Although we're not perfect at communicating, we've come a long way in understanding each other's dialect. And who knows? Once Elaine and I master this man-woman bilingual thing, we may tackle Swahili next.   *James Charis*

A STEP FURTHER

Translating Your Conversation

1. *If you're not sure what your mate means, simply ask.* When my wife says, "You never tell me anything," I try to have the sense to reply, "Help me understand what you mean." Then I attempt to keep my mouth shut until she's finished explaining.

2. *Remember that men usually want to hear the highlights; women, the details.* Hence, if you want the "Headline News" version of anything, ask me. If you want the "News Hour" account, talk to my wife.

3. *Watch body language.* Silence can be a perplexing mode of male communication for the female who is used to talking out problems. But instead of prying into a man's thoughts if he's brooding or bothered, discuss his feelings at *his* convenience— you'll be surprised what you learn!

JC

Faith Focus

What's your communication style as a couple? In what ways could you and your spouse become more "bilingual" in translating each other's speech and actions?

Prayer Pointer

Ask God to help you see your eyes and ears as gifts to use in discovering how best to "translate" your spouse's communication. Pray for your spouse—and that God will give you the love and patience you need to learn more about his "language."

HONOR THE LORD WITH YOUR
WEALTH AND WITH THE BEST PART
OF EVERYTHING YOUR LAND PRO-
DUCES. THEN HE WILL FILL YOUR
BARNS WITH GRAIN, AND YOUR
VATS WILL OVERFLOW WITH THE
FINEST WINE.

PROVERBS 3:9-10

*W*ho should pay bills?

- Who should carry—and balance—the checkbook?
- Who should be responsible for investments?
- Who should decide if a large item should be purchased—or not?

According to *Psychology Today*, use of money is one of the top three problems in marriage. And for Christians, the problem intensifies due to biblical commands to honor God with our resources (Prov. 3:9-10)—especially if husband and wife disagree on how much to give. So how can couples work together to make wise financial decisions?

Here's what works in other couples' marriages—and might work in yours.

Who's Minding the Money?

As newlyweds, my husband, Paul, and I wanted to avoid the friction we'd been warned could result from disagreements over money. Since we both worked full-time, we decided to experiment with a financial arrangement we copied from a missionary couple who were good friends of Paul's parents. After paying their bills, this couple divided their income in half. The wife, who believed in being frugal, saved as much of her half of the disposable income as she liked, and the husband, who believed in being charitable, donated as much of his half as he liked. They were able to meet their responsibilities without either spouse's significantly compromising his or her temperament.

Since Paul and I were used to managing our own finances and had radically different temperaments as well, this system appealed to us. After some discussion, we chose to adapt it a bit. Instead of pooling our income, we kept separate checking accounts and paid our joint bills on a percentage basis according to our respective salaries.

Since then, as our circumstances have changed, we've had to adjust our system a couple of times. For example, after we had children and I began working part-time, my income was drastically reduced. I figured out that after paying my percentage of the bills, small as it was, my personal spending money would barely cover the cost of a double-dip ice-cream cone! After experimenting with several variations on the separate checking-accounts system, we went with a simpler, more traditional arrangement: We now have one joint checking account from which Paul pays all the bills. It's less hassle, but I have to confess I'm nervous about giving up my financial "independence."

That's not surprising, because money issues tap into so many sensitive areas in marriage—power, control, self-esteem, gender roles, and spiritual values. Often the way couples feel about these things—and the way our varying church backgrounds influence our view of leadership in marriage—can impact the way we handle our money.

But Scripture offers general principles for good financial stewardship. For example, we're admonished to be charitable (Luke 6:30), to be content with what we have (1 Timothy 6:6-8), and to avoid loving money (1 Timothy 6:10). However, there aren't any clear-cut commands about who should handle money within a marriage— or how it should be done.

> *The Assurance that God can be trusted to provide what we need at the time we need it will keep us looking for his options—and will help us live joyfully on whatever he provides.*
>
> SANDY LARSEN

So who should mind the money in your marriage? According to all the couples I have talked with, there's no one right answer. Each couple has to craft an approach that best fits their temperaments, lifestyle, and ability to discipline themselves.

What's most important is that spouses agree on—and affirm their respective roles. Those roles may change over time as jobs, circumstances, and priorities shift. But as long as spouses work together, understand their gifts, and seek to be good stewards of the financial resources God has blessed them with, it's likely their money will be managed well.

Janis Long Harris

A Step Further

Money Sense

1. *Who likes to do it?* Consider your and your spouse's natural gifts and preferences.
2. *Who has the time?* Some couples divvy up money chores according to time or schedule flexibility. Other couples try to lighten the burden by sharing it.
3. *Who is most affected by it?* For instance, many women say their managing the checkbook makes sense when they're the ones making most of the day-to-day purchasing decisions.
4. *Who feels the need to control?* The most effective money-management systems give *both* spouses some control over how money is spent. You could agree on areas of primary decision making or agree to discuss any major purchases or money decisions together. Or you could divide up money and expenditures.   *JLH*

Faith Focus

How do you and your spouse handle money? Are you comfortable with the way in which you've chosen who does what? In thinking through your temperaments, personalities, gifts, time, etc., what changes could you make in your family's financial structure to help you grow closer as a couple?

Prayer Pointer

Thank God for his promises throughout Scripture to provide what you need, when you need it. Pray that he will keep you from worrying about your finances and that he'll give you and your spouse creative ideas for handling your family's finances.

Kiss me again and again, for your love is sweeter than wine. How fragrant your cologne, and how pleasing your name! . . . Take me with you. Come, let's run! Bring me into your bedroom.

Song of Songs 1:2-4

I don't know if we'll ever have sex again," a young mom told me in despair. "With two kids, we're so tired we fall asleep immediately."

She's not alone. A career-oriented couple recently admitted, "Sex is the last thing we think about after a long day in the office."

Yet, as married couples, sex is part of God's plan—and a wonderful part at that. Just dip into Song of Songs and read the sizzling snippets there!

Even in those tired and busy times of your marriage, you *can* have great sex.

Great Sex?!

It was the most romantic setting I could think of: fragrant candles flickered on both sides of our bed, the lights were turned low, and a bottle of Welch's sparkling grape juice awaited us. After a very busy season for both my husband and myself at work, we'd set aside our first "ordinary" night for a bedroom rendezvous.

Anticipation mounting, I did the dinner dishes, then slipped into my slinkiest negligee. Then, with a smile on my face, I sat down to await the arrival of my husbandly prince, who was in the garage fixing our car that had gone on the blink that morning.

I waited . . . and waited. Finally I plopped down on the bed to read a magazine. By the time Jeff came bounding up the stairs an hour later, grinning because the car was now back in good working order, he found me . . . asleep.

So much for planned romance!

If you're like us, life takes its toll on your sex life. So many things—work, church, home "roundtuits"—tug at your time. And then there are the people commitments—your family, friends, or children (if you have them). What wife hasn't wanted to kill whoever phones late at night? What mom hasn't dreamed of the time when a romantic mood wasn't interrupted to get a glass of water for a restless child? And what busy couple hasn't wished for even one night a week to be home alone?

For Jeff and me, tiredness and overcommitment can be real killers in our couple life. But those aren't the only sex-stoppers that many couples struggle with. Often past experiences loom so large for one partner (or both) that sex becomes something to be feared rather than antici-pated.

Take these friends (not their real names), for instance. Several years ago, Ida told me, "After my childhood sexual abuse, I find it difficult to be intimate." Tina shared, "I've al-ways worried about my weight. So when my boyfriend, Frank, wanted to go swimming, I panicked. No way was I going to let him see my body. Now that we're married, I still worry sometimes." John admitted, "The guilt of seeing por-nography as a teenager hangs over me every time I have sex with my wife." And Julie said, "When Rich and I had sex for the first time on our honeymoon, I cried. I wish I would have saved my virginity for him."

A good marriage relationship is the foundation of a good sexual relationship.

DR. BARBARA CHESSER

But even with the pain of their past, these couples have worked hard to keep sex as an enriching part of their couple life. Ida and her husband and John and his wife got help from a Christian counselor. Tina's concerns about weight were put to rest when Frank whistled appreciatively and said, "Honey, I think you're really sexy!" And Julie stated recently, face glowing, "I never knew sex could be so wonderful. Rich and I are a team in every way—and we give God the glory!"

As part of God's plan for married couples, sex is a won-derful reward. Are you treating it as such?

Ramona Cramer Tucker

A Step Further

Hints for Sizzling Sex

1. *Plan the time.* If not planned for, sex is easily set aside because of tiredness or a too-busy schedule.
2. *Set the stage.* An old adage says, "Sex starts in the kitchen." Treating each other with respect, love, and tenderness at all times will improve your intimacy.
3. *Get yourself in the mood.* Do what makes you feel sexy—take a relaxing, fragrant bath; light a candle; put on romantic music; leave work an hour early to get your hair done.
4. *Turn off the phone.* Or let your answering machine get it, if you have one. Anyone who has to reach you will call back.
5. *Read Song of Songs together.* Discussing love and sex as God created them will improve your communication—and can actually put you in the mood!   RCT

Faith Focus

On a scale of one to ten, how would you rate your sex life? How would your husband rate it? What can you do to make the time and take the opportunity to enjoy this wonderful, God-given gift in your marriage?

Prayer Pointer

Thank God for the marvelous gift of sex within marriage. Ask God to reveal to you ways in which you can make time together a priority—even if it means putting aside other outside activities.

How we praise God, the Father of our Lord Jesus Christ, who has blessed us with every spiritual blessing in the heavenly realms because we belong to Christ. He has showered his kindness on us, along with all wisdom and understanding.

EPHESIANS 1:3, 8

I worked for the same company for ten years—and they laid me off with no warning. What do I do now?"

Such words can strike fear into the heart of any family. Work not only pays the bills but also forms part of who we are. The concept of fulfilling work goes all the way back to Genesis 2, where God told Adam to "tend and care for" the Garden of Eden. So when unemployment hits home, how can we see God's blessings and tap into his wisdom (Eph. 1)? Meet one family who turned their recession into closer relationships—and a deeper faith.

When Unemployment Hits Home

We were living the American Dream—and we never thought it would end. My husband and I had a three-bedroom house in the suburbs, two cars, and plenty of credit at our disposal. If I wanted a new dress or handbag, I bought it without hesitation. Since my husband, a regional sales manager with a large corporation, traveled about five days a week, a trip to the mall also eased the loneliness I felt. Neither of us liked his extensive travel, but we liked what his paychecks could buy—the opportunity for me to care for our two young sons at home and a seemingly secure future—complete with college educations for our children and a retirement of leisure.

But one morning, I heard my husband walking down the hall when he was supposed to have left on a business trip.

"What'd you forget, hon?" I called.

"I had a meeting at the office early. They just laid me off." His lips trembled. His job level was being eliminated, and he and another regional sales manager were out of a job.

I was shocked. He had been with the company for more than thirteen years, and his work had been exemplary.

"Why is this happening?" I wanted to scream at God. *Layoffs happen to others, but not to hardworking Christian men like my husband,* I thought—as though being a Christian were a ticket to financial prosperity. A hatred for those who decided my husband's fate lodged deep in my heart.

As the recession deepened and the months passed, I became more discouraged and frightened. Our savings dwindled. My husband had good days, when he'd look for jobs, and bad days, when he wouldn't get out of bed until noon.

Then one day I found Proverbs 30:8-9: "Give me neither poverty nor riches! Give me just enough to satisfy my needs. For if I grow rich, I may deny you and say, 'Who is the Lord?'" I recalled the times God had provided manna for the Israelites as they wandered in the desert, giving them just enough to meet their daily needs and strengthen their faith.

God is using this career pitfall to call our family closer to him! I realized. *This layoff is part of his plan. If we look for them, we'll see God's blessings.* The anger I had felt toward my husband's boss began to melt. I asked God to forgive me for my worry and impatience toward my husband. And I began looking for the blessings God was giving us.

> *The Bible is full of examples of God's children facing hard times—and God's faithfulness and provision throughout them.*
> JUDI LIGHT

Eleven months later, my husband found work at a company that encourages family values and appreciates his efforts. He enjoys his new job much more than the old one. Best of all, we're home together in the evening to share a real family life, something that was almost nonexistent with his previous job.

I've discovered we have something much better than the American Dream—a God who loves us and guides us to true spiritual prosperity. *Annie Oeth*

A STEP FURTHER

Looking at the Upside of Down

1. *Spend time as a couple doing what you enjoy.* Remember—walks and talks are free entertainment. And they reap lasting rewards!
2. *Make the most of time off work by getting to know your kids better.* Have a romp in a pile of leaves; push them on a swing; put together a family scrapbook.
3. *Redefine socializing.* If it used to mean going out for dinner, stay home instead. Make popcorn or a dessert and play Trivial Pursuit.
4. *Use the time for ministry.* Other people are in your shoes, too. Encourage them, and you'll find a natural support group.
5. *Grow closer to God.* Pour over his Word and pray diligently as you examine possible job options. Ask him to help you be creative in your solutions.   AO

Faith Focus

Has your spouse gone through unemployment—or a
period of dissatisfaction with his job? How have you
handled such a time—individually and as a couple?
What steps can you take together to help you not only
survive but also *thrive* in times when his job or your job
is either nonexistent or unfulfilling?

Prayer Pointer

Ask the Lord to reveal to you and
your spouse ways in which your
husband can find satisfaction—
either by leading him to a new
job, by providing opportunities at
his old job, or by revealing areas
aside from work where he could
use his talents.

WE CAN MAKE OUR PLANS, BUT

THE LORD DETERMINES OUR STEPS.

PROVERBS 16:9

DAY 10

*M*y family moved frequently when my sister and I were young: from London, Ontario, to New York, Colorado, Iowa, Montana, and Saskatchewan, Canada. Whew! That's a lot of transitions. But my parents believed wholeheartedly in Proverbs 16:9—they wanted to go where the Lord directed them. Through all those moves, they worked hard to assure my sister and me that we were safe in God's hands, no matter where we might travel.

If you're in the middle of moving—whether it's changing churches, houses, cities, or jobs—here's how to keep those changes in perspective.

Moving Frenzy

The new-house part of moving is always fun. Getting there is not. Consider filling a packing box the size of Delaware with sixties albums we never play but still know all the words to. Living in chaos for weeks on end. Hurling ourselves on the mercy of our friends: "What are you doing next Saturday?" Moving may test the best of friendships—but it really tests a marriage.

First, we had to pick out the house, which meant going out in the dead of winter with a three-year-old in tow ("Nobody's buying; it's a good time," our real estate agent counseled) and looking at residences ranging from "home with great potential" (read: *I've seen cleaner gerbil cages*) to an adorable white-frame house lived in by the same family for forty years.

But houses are funny: An attachment can grow. A bungalow that had been sitting forlornly on its corner lot for months, hoping someone would notice its For Sale sign, caught our eye. We went and looked at it—and looked again.

"Hmmm," I said finally. "I think this house wants us."

We bought.

We had two weeks between closing and occupancy. "I will not live with the paint in these rooms," I told my husband.

"It looks perfectly good to me," he said.

It's funny how a woman's bossy hormones seem to erupt when she's moving into a new house: *"Paint!"*

We moved toward the end of December. It snowed. Fritz drove a U-Haul that lurched across town. We were finished by late afternoon and sank down into the kitchen chairs (the only available seating), surveying the wreckage with the *Now what?* sort of glazed stare unique to those who've just moved. And then we sat some more. After a "supper" of tuna sandwiches, we emitted a few low moans and did the only sensible thing to do under such circumstances: tucked our daughter in and went to bed ourselves.

The next day dawned clear and bright. We'd vowed that despite the press of the move, we would make it to church. Unfortunately, we hadn't reckoned on several things—no shampoo, no razor, few clothes. We did get to church—and hoped no one would notice Fritz's stubble and my greasy hair.

> *Whatever our creative God leads you to do, do it*
> *with the right motive—obedience to God.*
>
> CAROLE MAYHALL

Diehards that we are, we grimly vowed not to rest until every box was unpacked and every stick of furniture aesthetically positioned. Our goal: to be ready for friends coming for New Year's Eve. This meant continuous, up-till-midnight, grinding labor. It meant little conversation beyond grunts of "Where do you want this?" and a strangled "Unhhh" as we signed more checks.

While moving may put a few dents in a marriage, fortunately, they aren't permanent. One morning after we'd gotten settled, Fritz and I bundled up and sat on our front steps, basking in our own little corner of creation. It felt good—even if creation's corner *did* need shoveling.

Elizabeth Cody Newenhuyse

A STEP FURTHER

Adjusting to Your Move

1. *Be patient with each other.* Everyone adjusts to change differently.
2. *Label boxes.* When you're packing, use a bold marker to write "kitchen," "bathroom," etc., on the boxes so you won't have one large unidentifiable heap. When unloading, put the boxes in the appropriate rooms.
3. *Work one room at a time.* Having one normal-looking room will give you a place to relax when you're feeling overwhelmed.
4. *Throw or give away what you don't need or use.* There's nothing more frustrating than moving junk that you don't know where to store.
5. *Pray.* Ask God to help you in this transition—and as you reach out to your new neighbors.

RCT

Faith Focus

Have you recently undergone—or are you currently in—a time of transition, such as relocating to a new area or starting a new job? How do you deal with change? How about your spouse? What can you do together to ease the transition?

Prayer Pointer

Thank God for always being with you, no matter what transitions you face. Ask him to give you courage to reach out in making new friends—and patience to deal with your spouse and all the details of your move.

THE HEARTFELT COUNSEL OF A
FRIEND IS AS SWEET AS PERFUME
AND INCENSE.

PROVERBS 27:9

*H*ave you ever so enjoyed an evening with another couple that you laughed yourself silly?

Whenever my husband, Jeff, and I spend time with our friends David and Annette, that's exactly what we do. And that's not the only thing. Those dear friends have been present—with prayer, listening hearts, and hugs—through our good and difficult times for the past thirteen years. They offer us, in just the right dosage, "the heartfelt counsel of a friend."

Are you too busy to cultivate "couple" friends? Then here's why you should: because they're good for you—and your marriage.

Four of a Kind

My husband, Paul, and I love each other. We enjoy each other's company and have what I consider a strong marriage. We often wish we had more time alone. But we've discovered that time together isn't all we need for a satisfying marriage. We also need friendships with other couples.

As I think about it, some of the best times in our marriage have been spent with friends: playing knockdown, drag-out tennis with a couple whose lack of skills matched ours; getting together every year with another couple to celebrate a mutual wedding anniversary; or just "hanging out" with friends on a Friday night, sharing pizza and conversation.

But finding and maintaining those "couple" friendships isn't always easy. First, there has to be a four-way match. More than once, after an evening of socializing with another couple, I've said, "That was really enjoyable," and Paul has remained pointedly silent. Or the roles have been reversed.

Sometimes, spouses' differing expectations about friendship can be an obstacle. One spouse may enjoy more time alone than another or prefer a smaller friendship circle. Time and children are also barriers to couple friendships. And then there's the problem of attrition. Paul and I have felt a real void when some of our best friends have moved away. But even friends who stick around can change so much that you no longer share common interests.

Yet despite these barriers, Paul and I have chosen to go after couple friendships. The fun and satisfaction we find with other couples have been a definite plus in our relationship. And after conducting an informal survey, I've found the same is true of the many married people we know.

Why? Because friendships can actually enhance your relationship with your spouse. Friends can meet needs or share interests a spouse can't. "Sometimes your friends can give you an entirely fresh perspective on a problem," says Linda, who's been married to Len for eleven years.

Being with friends also can bring out positive qualities in a spouse that don't always come through in daily life. "When we're with another couple or a group of friends," says one wife I know, "Bob can have a very quick humor that he doesn't necessarily use with me. I'll think, *Boy, he's really funny.*"

> *Friendship is not a luxury, a nice but expendable extra. For the Christian, it's a biblical necessity.*
>
> ELIZABETH CODY NEWENHUYSE

Friends also can provide a sense of community in an increasingly individualistic society. "Friends add a new forum for talking through issues," observes one college professor, "and the pure fun of being with other human beings."

Friends bring serendipity into our lives. Although chances are you're more likely to become friends with people with whom you share a neighborhood, age bracket, church, or work situation, it doesn't always happen that way. One young couple I know of became best friends with a couple almost twenty years their senior—despite few outward common circumstances. Their advice to other couples: If you stick too rigidly to your categories, you can miss some great new friendships! *Janis Long Harris*

A STEP FURTHER

Cultivating Friendship

1. *Actively seek out friendships.* Don't wait for friendships to "happen." Invite others over to get to know them better.
2. *Seek out couples who share your values and interests.* Volunteer your help at a food pantry or sign up to sing in the church choir.
3. *Nurture the friendships you already have.* Take the initiative: Suggest plans for getting together. Send your friends a note telling them what their friendship means to you. Model the kind of friendship you'd like to have in return.
4. *Don't expect all your friendships to be mutual.* Remember that it's good to get together individually with friends, too.
5. *Mourn your lost friendships; then move on.* Don't let the loss prevent you from making new ones.

JLH

Faith Focus

Have you and your spouse ever discussed your friendship needs? Do you have any close couple friends you can count on (and who can count on you) to help each other grow closer to God? What "friendship" steps could you take to reach out to another couple over the next few months?

Prayer Pointer

Thank God for the friends you have in your life. Ask God to make you willing to overcome the obstacles to couple friendship and courageous enough to take a risk.

Now glory be to God! By his mighty power at work within us, he is able to accomplish infinitely more than we would ever dare to ask or hope. May he be given glory in the church and in Christ Jesus forever and ever through endless ages. Amen.

Ephesians 3:20-21

$\mathcal{Y}$our husband doesn't seem interested in going to church—or attends church sporadically. Or maybe a group of his friends has started a Bible study and he always finds other projects to do during that time. Or you know the Bible on his nightstand is growing dusty because he doesn't read it anymore.

When your faith is growing and your husband's isn't, don't give up. As Ephesians 3 says, God is "able to accomplish infinitely more than we would ever dare to ask or hope." Here's how to break the spiritual deadlock in your marriage.

Is There a Stale Mate in Your Marriage?

"He said what?" My voice registered shock.

The woman flushed and repeated her statement. "My pastor suggested I stop growing spiritually. If I don't, I'll be too far ahead of my husband, and that wouldn't be good."

Women whose husbands lag behind them in spiritual growth sometimes resort to a variety of methods to prod their husbands into a closer walk with Christ: giving mini-sermons to the children in front of the husband, nagging him about attending men's prayer breakfasts, telling children to review their Sunday school lessons with Dad.

How *should* you respond to the frustrating and painful situation of a less spiritually mature and passive husband who won't take spiritual leadership in the home? How can you encourage him to grow without creating bad feelings or resistance?

Grow as fast as you can. To stop growing yourself certainly is not the answer! That advice violates 2 Peter 3:18, which commands every believer to "grow in the special favor and knowledge of our Lord and Savior Jesus Christ." For any wife who finds herself spiritually out of sync with her husband, this means quiet, unobtrusive digging into the Word, time spent in prayer, and counsel from older, more experienced women.

Show, don't tell. Ask God for creative ideas on how your particular husband might see Christ in you. Husbands who become on fire for Christ later than their wives say it is because they saw their wives respond to difficult situations in a Christlike way.

Look for ways to respect your husband—even when he

doesn't earn respect. I'm so glad God never gives us a command he doesn't give us the power to do (Eph. 3)! So actively look for things to respect about your husband, rather than concentrate on the twenty things you don't respect him for.

Refuse to usurp your husband's leadership. If you assume the responsibility (unless your husband has specifically delegated a responsibility, such as reading a nighttime Bible story) for decisions regarding your children, your home, or your finances, you may be hindering your husband's ability to take spiritual leadership in the family.

> *God has a plan and a purpose for each season of our life. We must trust in his timing for the change of our life seasons and learn to rejoice within them.*
> BARBARA J. DOLL

Be a fun, joyful person. Of all people, God's children should have a joyful and merry heart, with laughter lurking below the surface, erupting often (see Prov. 17:22). Yes, we have heavy burdens. But we also have a Burden Bearer. If we take those burdens to the Lord, we find our burdens light (Matt. 11:28-30).

During the turbulence of living with a passive believer, it's difficult to remember who controls the wind and waves. True, God won't force his will upon a husband, but he will bring mighty forces to bear in order to speak peace to a situation. We can't program his methods or his timing in our spouse's spiritual journey. What we can do, however, is obey God when he tells us to love and honor our husband.

Carole Mayhall

71

A Step Further

Praying for Your Husband

1. *Commit five minutes a day to pray just for him.*
2. *Pray a different Scripture for him each month.* For instance, pray through Colossians 1:9-11 for three days:
   - Day 1: Ask God to help you understand what he wants to do in your lives.
   - Day 2: Ask him to make you spiritually wise.
   - Day 3: Ask to live in a way that honors and pleases the Lord.
3. *Pray for specific requests God puts on your heart:* that your husband develops a friendship with a committed Christian who will challenge him, that he turns his attention to the Bible instead of television sitcoms or computer games.
4. *Thank God!* Write down the answers to prayer when they come and date them.

CM

Faith Focus

Have you—or your husband—ever faced a "stale mate" situation in your marriage? If so, what did you do about it? If this reflects your current circumstances, how can you encourage your spouse (or yourself) to grow in faith?

Prayer Pointer

Ask God to give you *and* your spouse a hunger to study his Word and the passion to live out your faith in your family, your community, your church. Thank God for the ways he's already helped you grow.

I WILL MAKE YOU MY WIFE FOR-
EVER, SHOWING YOU RIGHTEOUS-
NESS AND JUSTICE, UNFAILING
LOVE AND COMPASSION. I WILL BE
FAITHFUL TO YOU AND MAKE YOU
MINE.

HOSEA 2:19-20

*H*e used to be so romantic," Aimee told me. "Now I'm lucky to get flowers on Valentine's Day. Sometimes I wonder if it's because I gained weight after I had the kids. Does he no longer find me attractive?"

It's inevitable that our bodies begin to settle a bit over the years. But what does that changing body mean to your husband? Will he still find you as attractive as he did the day you got married?

Get ready for a real guy's perspective on his wife's body—and the "forever" vows in Hosea.

If Fitting Rooms Could Talk

After sixteen years of marriage, I've learned there are some things about my wife that will probably never change. She'll always leave the family car with less than a tenth of a tank of gas, and she'll *always* need another pair of shoes to go with the skirt she borrowed.

But even more certain than gas fumes and assorted heels is the assurance that when beach weather approaches, Judy, my lovely wife with eyes that could make a *Glamour* girl envious, will be on some sort of diet.

For the life of me, I can't figure where my beautiful wife learned to equate bathing suits with certain medieval torture. But I do know her agony over body image is real—as it is for most American women past puberty who assume that they're overweight.

I experienced Judy's "body panic" firsthand when we recently went shopping for a new bathing suit.

"Well, hon, what do you think?" my wife-turned-fitting-room-model asked warily.

"I think you look beautiful, sweetie. I could eat you up!"

"I don't look like Tubby the Tuba, do I?" she asked, poking at every part of her anatomy. "I need to lose ten pounds."

"You look great."

"Well, I'll think about it." Translation: "I'm fat." And back went the accursed garment on the rack.

Such conversations highlight the fact that the way Judy sees herself and the way I see her are two different ways of seeing. Truth be told (and it will never be told by advertisers or your local fitness center), the search for the perfect body is over before it begins. In my own lifetime, Marilyn Monroe gave way to Twiggy, who gave way to Bo Derek, who gave way to . . . In the end, what you're left with is what you started with—the body God gave you. Which is really good news. Really.

Frankly, all those women in *Vogue* and *Glamour*—you know who I'm talking about—are perfectly boring. How else would you describe someone who looks like everyone else?

But no one looks like Judy. Her eyes? Warm, bright, and alive. Her smile? Supportive, friendly. Am I saying I'd choose my wife over the woman promising me an Obsession night? You bet I would. And part of my role as a husband is to make sure Judy understands this every day of our marriage. It is my privilege to help Judy see herself as she really is—to praise her God-given assets.

> *Aging is a matter of fact. Love and maturity,*
> *on the other hand, are a matter of choice.*
> CHARLES R. SWINDOLL

That's not to say Judy will ever enjoy shopping for swimwear. But at least she knows she doesn't have to compete with the women in *Vogue* for my attention or her self-worth. She is free to fine-tune her dieting for health's sake.

It's now four weeks into Judy's latest diet, and she triumphantly announced tonight that a few precious pounds have been shed. I applaud her willpower. But our two sons seem only mildly impressed.

"You're already the most beautiful mom in the world," they say.

Take that, *Glamour* girl.   *Harold B. Smith*

A Step Further

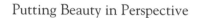

Putting Beauty in Perspective

1. *Realize we all grow older.* Do you expect to look the same as you did when you were a teenager? If so, give yourself a reality check.

2. *Remember, no one compares to you.* If you struggle with self-esteem, don't make it a practice to buy or read magazines with glamorous cover models.

3. *Highlight your uniquenesses.* If you have beautiful eyes, play them up. If your hair is your best feature, get a new haircut that frames your face.

4. *Focus on your physical and spiritual health, rather than on what your body is—or isn't.* That way, if you *do* lose weight, you're more likely to keep it off—and you'll be a more joyful person to be around, too!

5. *Read what God says about you in his Word.* Try Psalm 139 for starters.   RCT

Faith Focus

How do you feel about your body? your husband's body? Do you compare yourself or your husband to magazine cover models or younger, sexier-looking friends or coworkers? In what ways can you make the best of your body's features?

Prayer Pointer

Ask God to help you discern what's realistic from what's unrealistic in your expectations of yourself. Thank him for the unique body he's made "so wonderfully complex" (Psalm 139:14) and given to you—even though it's not perfect!

TRUST IN THE LORD WITH ALL
YOUR HEART; DO NOT DEPEND ON
YOUR OWN UNDERSTANDING.
SEEK HIS WILL IN ALL YOU DO,
AND HE WILL DIRECT YOUR PATHS.

PROVERBS 3:5-6

I feel so lonely."

- "I wish my husband would go to church with me."
- "How can I love God *and* my husband when he's against Christianity and I'm a Christian?"

If you're married to an unbeliever, you may have said (or thought) these words. You wonder how much to say (or not say) and whether to risk inviting him to Bible study.

In turbulent times, Proverbs 3:5-6 offers comfort for spiritually mismatched couples and all those who care about them: if you depend on God, "he will direct your paths."

Following is counsel from someone who's been there.

When You're Spiritually Mismatched

Six words sum up the role God played during the early years of my marriage to Leslie: *He just wasn't on our agenda.* After we married in 1972, we were both busy with our careers, starting our family, and buying a house. Frankly, there was no room for God—even if he did exist. Leslie and I were best friends and for the most part didn't have any worries.

But our happiness went into a skid in fall 1979, when Leslie decided to follow Jesus Christ. She had been introduced to him through the gentle witness and friendship of a woman whose daughter was the same age as ours. Leslie's decision initiated the most tumultuous era of our relationship.

When Leslie met new people at church and became enthused by their spirituality, I felt hurt and devalued. I was afraid her respect for me would dwindle because I wasn't committed to God.

I was also afraid she'd become a wild-eyed religious fanatic—embarrassing me in front of my buddies, spilling details about our private life in her prayer group, rejecting our old friends.

And I was frustrated because, for the first time in our relationship, our values were at odds. When Leslie wanted to give money to the church, I blew my top (even though she got a part-time job just so she could contribute). I felt I'd married one Leslie and now she was changing into someone I hadn't bargained for. I wanted the old Leslie back!

Looking back now, I realize that the more Leslie tried to live out the Christian life—with purity, integrity, honesty, tolerance, and forgiveness—the more obvious it became that my life was corroded with cynicism, bitterness, super-ficiality, and self-centeredness. I could see who I really was.

The Bible calls this being convicted of sin. It made me angry because I didn't want to face my sin. I wanted to re-main "spiritually neutral"; meanwhile, Leslie grieved over what was missing in our marriage.

If you and your spouse are spiritually mismatched, there's hope. God won't abandon you. He'll offer you wis-dom on how to survive. He can take your heartbreaking ex-perience of living with an unbeliever and mold you into someone whose faith has depth, character, and quality

As Christians, we're here to learn how to love God and trust him. Our highest calling is to be a walking advertisement for his incredible power and attributes.

MICHELE HALSEIDE

Leslie's and my spiritual mismatch has a wonderful end-ing. Two years later, after much searching and investiga-tion, I accepted Christ. But not every husband and wife end up together in God's kingdom. I know a woman who's been praying for her unbelieving husband for sixteen years, and he only recently agreed to come to church with her.

Remember, you are not held accountable by God if your spouse rejects Christ. So don't let misplaced guilt wear you down. Your responsibility is to live out your life, as best you can, in a Christ-honoring way. As a fellow pas-tor says, "If you honor God with your everyday life, he'll honor you for a lifetime"—even in the midst of a spiritual mismatch.

Lee Strobel

A STEP FURTHER

Tips for Turbulent Times

1. *Harness others' support.* Two are better than one (Eccles. 4:9).
2. *Exercise restraint.* Forcing Christianity down your spouse's throat is counter-productive.
3. *Live out your faith.* Instead of debating with your spouse about who God is, let Jesus change your character, attitude, and outlook. As you're transformed into a better person, your spouse may become more open-minded about your faith.
4. *Pray, pray, and pray.* When you're feeling hurt, frustrated, angry, and afraid, who but God can really help? For starters, focus your prayers on Ezekiel 36:26.
5. *Love your spouse even when he isn't very lovable.* Wait for God's timing, even when you desperately want to take matters into your own hands.   LS

Faith Focus

If you're married to an unbeliever, do you have a mature Christian friend who can give you support, guidance, and encouragement? If not, what steps can you take to find one? How can you show love and kindness to your unbelieving spouse?

Prayer Pointer

Thank God for the sacrifice of his Son and for how it brought joy and hope into your life. Pray for your spouse—that he will grow more and more open to the gospel. Pray for yourself—that you will be wise in your words and loving in your actions.

MANY WATERS CANNOT QUENCH LOVE; NEITHER CAN RIVERS DROWN IT. IF A MAN TRIED TO BUY LOVE WITH EVERYTHING HE OWNED, HIS OFFER WOULD BE UTTERLY DESPISED.

SONG OF SONGS 8:7

$\mathcal{W}$e all have times when we feel as though we've fallen "out of love" with our spouse. Whether it's because of hurts we've nurtured through the years over forgotten anniversaries or birthdays or because of a spouse's workaholism, that well of romantic feeling runs dry. Let's face it: Marriage is work—and it's not always easy. But during those desert times, it's good to remember one of the sizzling phrases from Song of Songs: "Many waters cannot quench love."

The next time you've had it with your husband, here's how you can fall in love with him . . . again.

Falling in Love with Your Husband . . . Again

It was Valentine's Day. As I searched row after row of cards, I grew more depressed. Each sentiment painted a picture of what was missing in my marriage.

When I married David twenty years ago, I thought we'd grow together in every way—spiritually, emotionally, and physically. David told me he believed in God, but each Sunday, I ended up sitting in church alone. When David came home from work each day, I wanted to chat, but he wanted to watch the news. I wanted kids, and although David didn't, he agreed to one child after the car loan was paid off. Then an emergency hysterectomy dashed my hopes of motherhood.

Over the next ten years, David progressed in his career, and I found fulfillment in mine. While I was proud of my husband's success, the more he achieved, the less significant I felt. Too many missed communications, chilly silences, and unkind words led us further apart, and we even stopped making love.

Tears pooled in my eyes as I returned to my car empty-handed. Once home, I opened my Bible and found 1 Peter 3:1-2: "Your godly lives will speak to them better than any words. They will be won over by watching your pure, godly behavior."

How am I supposed to win David over by my behavior when my anger is so close to the surface? I anguished. But since I couldn't separate what God had joined (Matt. 19:4-6), I prayed, "Change me, Lord—I'll do whatever you ask."

Daily, the Lord began to show me little ways to warm up

the icy climate in our home—like celebrating David's half-birthday with half a cake, or simply thanking him for going to work every day. But touching—making that final sensory connection—scared me.

It had been two years since we'd made love. Seven times in a row I'd initiated lovemaking, only to be rejected. Now, in the midst of my fear, I felt the Lord's gentle leading: *Start at the beginning.* So I touched David's arm when we talked or placed my hand on his back.

Marriage is a series of phases, where we can fall "in" and "out of" love. During the times we're not feeling in love, we must hold fast to our wedding vows and trust God to preserve our relationship.
SUSAN ASHTON

After several days of "thawing," I made my move. "David, I need a hug." Our first attempt was stiff, almost awkward. But each day I asked for and received these revitalizing moments of warmth. Then one day, I turned around to find David's waiting arms poised for a hug.

One ordinary Saturday, David grabbed my hand and looked at me with tender, pleading eyes. As we embraced, forgiveness melted our hearts. Apprehensions, awkwardness, and old hurts vanished. The timing, the place, the circumstance—all had been orchestrated by God. We came together as naturally and comfortably as when we were first married, and completed the final step in our journey back to each other.

Now when I search the racks for a valentine, I breathe a quick thanks to the One who's renewing the romance in our once-arid marriage. *C. C. Brooks*

A Step Further

Livening Up Your Romance

1. *Think about your dating days.* What made your then-boyfriend feel special? Relive a favorite picnic. Dress up. Play romantic music.
2. *Find new ways to please your spouse.* Watch a football game with him, or make a special meal and set the table for two. Deliver flowers to his work, or buy him a balloon and tie it to his car just to say "I love you."
3. *Whisk him away for a special treat.* Keep your destination a surprise.
4. *Don't underestimate the value of a hug—or a smile.* It's the little things that add up to intimacy!
5. *Pray for yourself and your husband.* Continue to walk in obedience to God's Word, and he'll provide everything you need (Matt. 6:33). CCB

Faith Focus

Has there been a time when you've fallen out of love with your spouse? If so, what did you do during that time? If you need to fall in love *again*, which of the "Ways to Liven Up Your Romance" could you try?

Prayer Pointer

Thank God for that early rush of love you felt for your husband while dating. Ask God to renew your passion and desire for your husband—and to help you be creative in your expressions of love toward him.

EACH MAN MUST LOVE HIS WIFE
AS HE LOVES HIMSELF, AND THE
WIFE MUST RESPECT HER HUS-
BAND.

EPHESIANS 5:33

*W*hat makes your spouse happy? A back rub? A love note in his lunch? A night away to see an action movie with his guy friends? A homemade "appreciation certificate" for completing your garage cleanup?

Ephesians 5:33 tells us to "respect" our husband, and just obeying that command could keep us busy for a lifetime. But what would happen if we not only respected and loved our spouse but also *cherished* him—made him feel special? If you want your marriage to grow more intimate, here's how to figure out what your man loves best.

Cherishing Your Spouse

"Are you picking your husband up at the airport this afternoon?" I asked my friend, whose husband was returning from a weeklong business trip.

"No," she replied, "I didn't want to disturb the baby's nap, so I arranged for a coworker to get him."

"How will that make your husband feel?" I asked.

"He's not too happy about it," she admitted, "but that's just the way it is."

If my friend's husband were honest about his feelings, I'm certain he would say he didn't feel very important to his wife that day. And if we were to watch a video of our own life, I'm afraid we'd often wince at the frequency with which we prefer ourselves or others over time with our husband. Somehow, over the years, while we still love our spouse, we often forget the importance of *cherishing* him.

The truth is, men and women define *cherish* differently. To me, it means feeling cared for in special ways, being protected and treasured. I know my husband, Jack, loves me. But I feel cherished when he says, "I don't want you driving in this fog—I'll take you," or, "Let me carry that—it's too heavy for you." I feel cherished when he takes my arm as we cross a busy street, changes the oil in my car, says, "I couldn't live without you," or gives me an impractical but special gift.

But Jack would probably raise an eyebrow at "protection," give grudging assent to "being cared for," and look bewildered at "treasured." For many men, the word *cherish* holds little identification. Oh, sure, men like to be cared for when they're sick, sympathized with when they're discouraged, pampered when they're tired. But what really makes them feel special may be a little less predictable.

One morning, while we were having breakfast at a coffee shop with some friends, the question of cherishing came up. One of the husbands considered the question seriously, paused a moment, then said thoughtfully, "I don't feel cherished when my wife questions my motives; when she doesn't give me the benefit of the doubt; when she assumes that she knows the reason behind what I do and, in her eyes, it's wrong, or different, from what she would do. I feel prejudged when that happens."

> *Every human needs to feel valued, significant, and worthwhile.*
> NYLA JANE WHITMORE

While the word *love* makes up the marriage painting, the ways we cherish each other add the beautiful strokes of color to its canvas. A marriage can probably get by without it—but how much more vivid and dynamic our marriage will be with it! God gives us this command: "Most important of all, continue to show deep love for each other, for love covers a multitude of sins" (I Pet. 4:8). If cherishing is part of that love—and I'm convinced it is—then the God who empowers you with his Holy Spirit will give you the ability to both love *and* cherish your husband. So how will you go about cherishing him today?   *Carole Mayhall*

A Step Further

Cherish Is the Word

1. *Pray for wisdom (James 1:5).* Look up verses for your particular situation.
2. *Ask questions.* "Honey, how would you like me to respond when you're discouraged—to sympathize silently, leave you alone, or try to cheer you up with an activity or funny story?"
3. *Build an atmosphere of caring.* Each week, share with him one quality that you admire. Express respect, praise, and love.
4. *Study his response to what you do.* For instance, he may prefer your cancelling a social engagement when he's "peopled out" to *I Love You* spelled out in M&M's on his pillow.
5. *Think deeds.* Words are important, but for the significant man in my life, cherishing is heard more loudly through actions— like fixing his favorite meal.   CM

Faith Focus

What makes your man feel treasured? If you don't know, go on a "treasure hunt," using the tips in "Cherish Is the Word." What one thing can you do (or not do) to cherish your spouse over the next month?

Prayer Pointer

Thank God for creating your spouse as a unique individual and for bringing you together in marriage. Ask God to help you as you build an atmosphere of caring in your home — and discover fresh ways to cherish your husband!

GOD BLESSES THOSE WHO ARE
MERCIFUL, FOR THEY WILL BE
SHOWN MERCY. GOD BLESSES
THOSE WHOSE HEARTS ARE PURE,
FOR THEY WILL SEE GOD.

MATTHEW 5:7-8

$\mathcal{H}$ave you ever said or heard the following:

- "You never listen to me!"
- "You're stubborn—just like your parents."
- "You'll never change—you're a loser!"

How sad that in the heat of marital battle we say words we'd rarely—if ever—say to our friends. It's the old "familiarity breeds contempt" adage at work.

But instead of nasty words, anger, and bitterness, God calls us to be merciful—and gives the merciful his blessing. When you and your spouse don't agree, here's how to reach out with the gift of mercy.

Dealing with Disagreement

I was thirty-two when I literally bumped into Jim at church. Embarrassed, we both said, "I'm sorry," then laughed. That brief encounter led to coffee and conversation at a restaurant.

It didn't take long for my heart to fall in love with Jim. Both somewhat shy, neither of us had dated much. Jim was gentle, sensitive toward my needs, encouraging, and attentive. Over the next several months, our bond deepened when we discovered we both came from non-Christian families.

Then, six months later, we got married. Trouble brewed the first morning of our honeymoon in the Bahamas. We couldn't seem to agree on where we wanted to go for breakfast or what we wanted to do for the day. As Jim probed, asking about my thoughts and feelings, I got angry. *After all,* I thought, *why can't he just decide and let me relax?* I was tired after all the wedding preparations.

It got worse. By the end of our two-week honeymoon, Jim had withdrawn. Desperate to evoke a response from him, I yelled at him. After all, that's the way my mom gets my dad to respond.

Our fights escalated after our honeymoon, turning into ugly, name-calling arguments. Only three months into our marriage, I thought, *Lord, why is marriage so hard? We can't agree on anything anymore—what happened to all those things we held in common?*

Not long after that, my husband hesitantly approached me as I did dishes in the kitchen. "Anna, I need to talk with you." When I looked up, startled he was even talking, he continued, "I love you, and I want us to have a good marriage. But we've gotten off on the wrong foot. Can we talk?" As he began to pour out his thoughts and feelings, I discovered a lot about my husband's background. He had lived in a home where no one yelled when they disagreed; they just backed away and pretended there wasn't a problem. My family disagreed vigorously and loudly—and often.

God's love for us and mercy toward us make our love able to endure.

JILL BRISCOE

That night sparked a turnaround in our marriage. I was humbled by Jim's vulnerability in making the first move— and shamed by the way I'd been treating him. I'd gotten mired down in selfishly wanting things *my* way.

The next week, we made an appointment with our pastor, who then suggested a counselor. Over the next year, we met with that godly counselor to sort out our backgrounds, our responses to life situations, our differences and similarities. With his help, we learned positive ways of communicating through our disagreements instead of withdrawing or yelling.

Today Jim and I have been married fifteen years. We wouldn't trade those first months of pain for anything, because we learned so much about each other—and most of all about a mighty God who's always there, rooting for us. As Romans 8:31 says, "If God is for us, who can ever be against us?" Who indeed?   *Anna Matthews*

A STEP FURTHER

When You Disagree

1. *Count to ten before you open your mouth.* Think, *What effect will my words have?*
2. *Use I and we rather than you.* Don't say, "You make me so mad." Try, "When we're late to church, I feel as if we're saying worshiping together as a family isn't important."
3. *Never say* never *or* always. These words bring up the past and elevate the emotion. Instead, focus on the immediate problem.
4. *Confront wisely—and in love (Eph. 4:29).* Don't confront in front of others—even when it's difficult to keep silent.
5. *Love—and forbear.* Remember that your spouse has faults—and so do you. But you married each other!
6. *Forgive—then move on.* Extend to your spouse the unconditional forgiveness that God extends to you.   AM

Faith Focus

How do you and your spouse handle times of disagreement—by giving the cold shoulder, arguing verbally, calmly discussing both sides, or pretending it never happened? How could your communication become increasingly more merciful during such times?

Prayer Pointer

Ask the Lord to help you be merciful when you and your spouse disagree. Thank God for forgiving you once for all—even when you didn't deserve it. Ask him to show you ways in which you and your spouse can work together toward a more intimate, God-honoring union.

Fix your thoughts on what is true and honorable and right. Think about things that are pure and lovely and admirable. Think about things that are excellent and worthy of praise.

Philippians 4:8

$\mathcal{H}$e loves wearing cowboy hats; you hate the Western image.

- He plans three months ahead; you prefer to be spontaneous.
- He gets a kick out of driving his old rusty pickup; you gag on the gas fumes.
- He irons his underwear; you're lucky if you get your shirt ironed.

How do you handle your spouse's unique quirks? Do you grumble about them, or, as Philippians 4:8 says, do you "think about things that are excellent and worthy of praise"?

Here's how you can learn to appreciate, rather than depreciate, your and your spouse's quirks.

Married to Mr. Clean

As a long-suffering member of a silent minority, I've finally decided it's time to come out of the broom closet and respond to all those people who complain about the difficulty of living with a messy spouse. I have the opposite problem: I'm married to a neatnik.

When I was growing up, I never doubted that someday my knight in shining armor would come riding into my life. Little did I know that when he finally arrived, he'd turn out to be a combination of the White Knight and the Tidy Bowl Man.

I should have known better after I saw my future husband's spit-shined penny loafers, finely pressed chinos, and the mirrorlike finish on his '58 green-and-white Chevy. And I shouldn't have been taken aback by his comment, a few weeks into our marriage, about the state of the top of the refrigerator. But I was. Who even looks at the top of the refrigerator?

So, early into our marriage, I learned to adapt. If I had spent my day sewing or shopping instead of cleaning, I put our vacuum cleaner in the middle of the floor, hid the dirty dishes in the oven, and sprayed a little lemon-scented furniture polish into the air. When "Mr. Clean" came home, I won the Good Housekeeping Seal of Approval!

Fortunately, our children understand their dad's penchant for cleanliness. They assume it's genetic. They've all participated in the annual Rites of Spring Cleaning at their grandmother's house. Every single item in her home is washed—dirty or not. No vase, doily, picture, windowpane, or wall escapes. You can't tell where you've stopped from where you've started—and the water in your pail never changes color!

Being married to Mr. Clean also means traveling with Mr. Clean. If the *Guinness Book of World Records* had a category called "Brief Motel Stays," we'd qualify. Once we hauled all our luggage into the room of a national chain before Mr. C. pulled down the bedspread, looked at the pillows, and announced, "We're checking out."

And we did.

> *Every healthy person grows and changes—*
> *and a healthy relationship is committed to adjusting*
> *to those growth spurts and the new dimensions*
> *they bring to life together.*
>
> VINITA HAMPTON WRIGHT

In restaurants, cleanliness takes precedence over cuisine. Silverware is carefully scrutinized, salt and pepper shakers checked for grease and fingerprints. My husband is presently trying to drum up support for a Constitutional amendment requiring all cooks and waitresses (and some waiters) to wear hairnets.

With missionary zeal, Mr. Clean carries his passion for the immaculate to the office. In his thinking, the real bottom line is how much dust is on the philodendron.

People who live together, it is said, tend to become more alike as time goes by. But can anyone absorb the characteristics of a neatnik just by living with him for years? I find it highly unlikely.

Well, I've been waiting for years to get this off my chest. I feel better already. And now, if you'll excuse me, I have to go wax the garage floor. *LaNelle C. Stiles*

A STEP FURTHER

Appreciating Your Spouse

1. *Accept each other's quirks.* Since you both have them, why not accept them as part of who your spouse is? That way you won't be as aggravated when they show up in daily life.

2. *Find out what makes your spouse tick.* If your checkbook is off by a penny and your spouse spends days worrying about it, gently ask him why that difference bothers him so much. You might receive an insight you'd otherwise never know about his background.

3. *Learn from your spouse.* If your spouse has a fetish about filing all your household bills in alphabetical order, he may have a point. Maybe they're easier to find and would save *you* hours of looking!

4. *Laugh together (but never at each other) about your foibles.* God-given humor makes any situation lighter! RCT

Faith Focus

What do you find quirky about your spouse? about yourself? How can you appreciate those quirks instead of letting them aggravate you?

Prayer Pointer

Thank your heavenly Father that he knew you in the womb and created you—and your spouse— just as you are! Ask him to help you focus on appreciating your husband instead of depreciating him.

DON'T LOSE SIGHT OF MY WORDS.
LET THEM PENETRATE DEEP
WITHIN YOUR HEART, FOR THEY
BRING LIFE AND RADIANT HEALTH
TO ANYONE WHO DISCOVERS THEIR
MEANING. ABOVE ALL ELSE,
GUARD YOUR HEART, FOR IT AF-
FECTS EVERYTHING YOU DO.

PROVERBS 4:21-23

I wish my husband left flowers on my car like hers does."

- "I wish he had a higher-paying job."
- "I wish he could laugh about fatherhood like Bill Cosby does."

With all the images of perfection being thrown at us from magazines, television, even chats with friends, it's no wonder we sometimes wish that our spouse were someone else. But for those "wishing" times, Proverbs 4 offers a caveat: "Above all else, guard your heart, for it affects everything you do."

So when you're tempted to compare your husband to someone else's, here's what to think about instead.

Why Can't He Be More Like . . . ?

Whenever I hear my friends' home-renovation stories, I always ask—knowing what their answer will be—"Did you do the work yourself?" "Oh yes," comes the airy response. "It was easy."

Sometimes I wish my husband were Bob Vila, formerly of *This Old House* fame. I wish he were as handy with a hammer as he is with a commentary. I wish my house looked like the "after" photos in *Better Homes and Gardens.*

I wish.

How many times have we all occasionally wished for a husband as spiritual as Billy Graham, as romantic as a soap-opera star, or as mechanical as Mr. Goodwrench? But for many women, this persistent "wanting-something-else" can take the shape of coveting someone else's spouse.

Such comparisons are dangerous because they dishonor our spouse (we're really saying we'd prefer to be married to someone else) and allow us to avoid responsibility for our own actions. Instead of resolving the discontent we may be experiencing in marriage, we take refuge in saying, "If only we could be like the Smiths." Naturally, we can't be, so we're absolved of our obligation to change.

Yet others' lives aren't necessarily better. "Everyone else's house looks better," says Dr. James Dobson, "because we all put on company manners when entertaining. If we were to drop in on someone unexpectedly, we might get quite a different picture!"

I know several couples whose marriages I admire. I know that my husband and I can learn from their positive models of mutual respect, playful affection, and shared spiritual commitment. But I've learned that the trick is to compare not mates but marriages. If I brood because I wish my husband could be like our friend Greg, who always takes his wife out, I'm edging toward dishonoring my spouse. But if I casually say, "Don't the Johnsons seem to have fun together? They went to that dinner theater—maybe we should go," I'm making a positive, nonthreatening suggestion.

When counselor Melissa McBurney struggles with disappointment over some aspect of her marriage, she tries to regain perspective. "I know for sure God wants me to be married to my husband, Louis," she says. "When you take that approach, everything else can be seen in a different light."

Marriages may be made in heaven, but people are responsible for the maintenance work.
BARBARA JOHNSON

As I write this, my bathtub drain is clogged, the hall needs painting, and there's an ugly vintage 1950s light fixture above our dining-room table. I would like my husband to take care of these things. But when I stood in the small white chapel of the church we grew up in, my knees shaking, and vowed to join my life with my husband's, a flawless house was not part of God's contract with us. Like Melissa, all I know is that God gave me this man—and this man only—to honor, to cherish, to enjoy. And instead of fretting about what he is not, I can celebrate what he is.

Elizabeth Cody Newenhuyse

A Step Further

Envy Busters

1. *Don't assume that someone else's life is better than your own.* Everyone has their own set of challenges.
2. *Adjust your expectations.* If you expect your spouse to be and do everything, you're bound to be disappointed.
3. *Be careful what images you allow into your mind.* Close the door on your fantasies; turn off the TV when you're feeling discontent.
4. *Give your spouse grace.* Study Scriptures about contentment and God's grace.
5. *Make the right kinds of comparisons work for your marriage.* Writer Mary Thomas Watts refers to older couples she knows who have served as "marriage mentors" for her and her husband. "They've made room for us in their lives," she writes, "letting us in on their foolishness and failures."   *ECN*

Faith Focus

Have you ever compared your husband to someone else's husband? If so, in what areas? In order to close the door on the comparison trap, which of the five "Envy Busters" could you try? How can you celebrate who your husband *is* instead of mourning over who he's not?

Prayer Pointer

Praise God for giving you your husband. Ask God to help you learn to celebrate who your husband is and all the good things he does. Ask the Lord to turn your thoughts homeward to solving any family problems and to keep you from envying others' relationships.

BE HUMBLE AND GENTLE. BE PATIENT WITH EACH OTHER, MAKING ALLOWANCE FOR EACH OTHER'S FAULTS BECAUSE OF YOUR LOVE.

EPHESIANS 4:2

$\mathcal{B}$ecause my mom loved to cook, clean, and decorate, I assumed that Sarah would, too, after we got married," my friend Randy told me. When I gently reminded him that Sarah had *never* done those things but was gifted in other areas, Randy sighed. "Yes, I know—and I love her. But I can't help but be a little disappointed."

If your spouse sometimes disappoints you in small or big ways, it's good to remember the command in Ephesians 4:2 to "be humble and gentle. Be patient." And, in the meanwhile, the next time your spouse begins to drive you nuts, try these suggestions.

Is Your Spouse Driving You Nuts?

I love bargains—so when I saw an exercise ski machine advertised in our Saturday paper for only $39.99, I couldn't resist. Since my husband, Dave, and I are among the myriad people who would like to firm up and drop ten pounds, it seemed perfect. We could lose weight together!

Dave was skeptical. But because I was so enthusiastic, he reluctantly said, "Why don't you check it out?"

Fast-forward to a couple of hours later, when most sane people on a Saturday morning are pouring their second cup of coffee and taking life easy. There Dave and I were—with hundreds of nuts, bolts, and parts carpeting our living-room floor. Dave struggled to follow the assembly directions in the sixteen-page instruction booklet, but by step eighteen, he knew we were in deep trouble. The needed screw was missing—and our irritation levels were rising.

While Dave has many talents, he isn't what I'd call "mechanically gifted," and his lack of ingenuity disappointed me. He silently wished that instead of bargain hunting, I'd just gone back to bed. Trying to assemble this ski-exerciser was giving us both a backache, and I wanted to cry instead of laugh. Dave wanted to junk it and write off the $39.99. Neither of us wanted to spend the rest of that Saturday looking for screws. What had started out as a great idea to draw us closer ended up making us irritated with each other.

Whether it's because that wonderful evening you planned for two gets wiped out by an unexpected flu bug, PMS clouds your usually sunny outlook on life, or your husband's habits are simply wearing you down, every marriage undergoes times when you and your spouse become disappointed with each other.

Usually we have the grace to love each other and handle the "biggies" that come along in life—a serious illness, the sudden loss of a parent, or a traumatic job change. But it's often those pesky little flies in the marital soup—chronic situations like battling over the thermostat or having a spouse who's always ten minutes late—that eat away at our relationship.

Why is disappointment a constant companion in most marriages? Blinded by the stars in our eyes, we often enter marriage with unrealistic expectations. Then we discover that the person we thought was perfect isn't—and he's married to another imperfect person. That's when disillusionment can set in.

> *We need to be as patient with each other*
> *as God is with us.*
> SUSAN ASHTON

But when we treat marriage as being for the long haul, it's one of the best testing grounds for living out our faith. We can allow those inevitable disappointments to gnaw at our marital contentment or use them to grow closer to each other and to God. When we base our marriage on biblical principles, give each other permission to be less than perfect, accept each other's shortcomings, and handle the little irritations and disappointments gracefully and with humor, we really do grow closer to each other. And what a bargain—we don't even have to pay $39.99! *Claudia Arp*

A Step Further

Dealing with Disappointments

1. *Realize you're married for life.* Leaving your family of origin (Gen. 2:24) to form a new family is not only an action but also an attitude. It's a daily calling to focus on each other and make other people and things less important.

2. *Name, don't blame.* If you're human, you'll become angry. Yet Scripture says, "Don't sin by letting anger gain control over you" (Eph. 4:26). Before you talk with your spouse about something he said or did, talk first with your heavenly Father and ask him to soften your attitude.

3. *Accentuate the positive.* Look for opportunities to affirm your husband and give him honest compliments.

4. *Lighten up.* If we can step back and not take ourselves so seriously, we may find something to laugh about.　　CA

Faith Focus

Has your spouse disappointed you in some way? If so, how? How do you look at those disappointments— as something that could tear your relationship apart or as opportunities to gain a new perspective about your husband? What positive qualities can you point out instead of those that drive you nuts?

Prayer Pointer

Thank God for loving you— even with all your foibles and quirky personality. Ask God to give you an unconditional love for your spouse, even when he disappoints you in some way. Ask God to reveal to you your spouse's positive qualities so you can encourage him.

Never let loyalty and kindness get away from you! Wear them like a necklace; write them deep within your heart. Then you will find favor with both God and people, and you will gain a good reputation.

Proverbs 3:3-4

*A*s Jeff and I sorted through his keepsake boxes after our wedding, he enthusiastically waved me over. "Check this out!" he said proudly. It was a fish head mounted on a plaque—a souvenir from a fishing trip he'd taken with his dad as a boy.

When he suggested we hang it above our bed, I balked. There was no way I'd wake up every morning to a fish! But, remembering the command to be kind in Proverbs, I suggested another option: his office (where it still has permanent residence).

If you're wondering what to do with your combined stuff, here's some perspective.

Married . . . with Antlers!

A mail-order company asked a sampling of brides, "What was the most challenging decorating item your new husband contributed to your married life?" Their answers won't surprise those of us who've been shoving boxes marked "His Stuff" around the attic for years: Deer antlers, stuffed fish, and weights reigned high on the list.

To be sure, there are men with a highly developed sense of home decorating, but sometimes their style leaves us cold. Suppose he wants ultramodern and you're into country. Will you toss fringed coverlets on his Danish modern sofa? Will he arrange your cast-iron roosters in a geometric pattern on the deck? Can this marriage be saved?

At our house, decorating was made easier because my husband, Bill, has the exact same response to every item on the furniture showroom floor: "That's fine." His lack of discernment in this arena revealed itself the first time I visited his apartment. It was . . . plaid. Fairly tidy, though, and that earned several points. Little did I know that in preparing for my visit, it took Bill several days to even find the floor.

Wisely, he kept the real showstopper among his collectibles out of sight on that first visit. Since Bill went to school for twelve years to earn his Ph.D. in Hebrew, his loved ones had all those years to save up and buy the perfect graduation gift for this godly young man: a Last Supper Talking Clock.

When Bill and I got engaged, it was time for me to meet The Clock. Three feet tall, battery operated, and voice activated, it features that famous painting of the Last Supper on velvet. In front of each apostle is a plastic candle. Every hour one of the candles lights up and from deep within the clock

comes a voice: "It's eight o'clock, and I am John. *BONG!*"
And then you hear soft music, eight chimes, and a verse of
Scripture.

I took one look at it and said what any self-respecting
woman would say: "Yard sale!"

Bill was crestfallen. So first we put it in the family room,
right over the couch. It didn't look too bad, and it certainly
was a conversation piece (in more ways than one). Problem
was, Bill was accustomed to the clock and I was not. So every
time one of the disciples started talking in the other room, I
yelled out, "Who is it?" "Andrew!" Finally we tipped the
clock on its side, carefully slid it in between the coats in the
hall closet, and forgot all about it.

> *What's precious to you may not be precious
> to someone else. So give each other some slack,
> laugh together, and come up with a mutual
> plan of what to do with your stuff.*
> RAMONA CRAMER TUCKER

Until one night. We had company over for dinner. One of
our friends stood close to the closet, tapped his watch, and
said, "What time is it, anyway?"

From back behind the coats, a muffled voice declared, "It's
seven-fifteen, and I am Peter. *BONG!*"

So, the next time you sigh as you watch your husband
dance through the door with yet another bowling trophy
for the china cupboard or a fresh set of antlers for the foyer,
take solace in this thought: At least they're quiet.

Liz Curtis Higgs

A STEP FURTHER

What to Keep—What to Throw

1. *How often do you use the item?* If you're keeping it around for that "someday" garage sale, plan the sale—or give it away.
2. *Could someone else really use it?* For instance, if you have two microwave ovens and you only use one, maybe a friend with less financial resources would appreciate your giving or lending it to her.
3. *Why are you keeping the item?* Is it laziness— you prefer not to clean out your closet? Security—you're afraid to let go of anything? Sentimentality—you want to pass it on to the next generation?
4. *Is it cluttering up your workspace?* If you have a food processor that adorns your kitchen countertop but is never used, get rid of it!

RCT

Faith Focus

How have you and your husband combined your stuff? Are there areas of your home that you need to declutter— in order to make cleaning easier or tempers cooler? How could you tackle your sorting on a doable schedule?

Prayer Pointer

Thank God for the things he's given you. Ask him to reveal to you what you should keep, store, throw away, or give away. Pray that God will help you focus on the things of eternity rather than the things of earth.

YOUR ATTITUDE SHOULD BE THE
SAME THAT CHRIST JESUS HAD.
THOUGH HE WAS GOD, HE DID
NOT DEMAND AND CLING TO HIS
RIGHTS AS GOD. HE MADE HIM-
SELF NOTHING; HE TOOK THE
HUMBLE POSITION OF A SLAVE
AND APPEARED IN HUMAN FORM.
AND IN HUMAN FORM HE OBEDI-
ENTLY HUMBLED HIMSELF EVEN
FURTHER BY DYING A CRIMINAL'S
DEATH ON A CROSS.

PHILIPPIANS 2:5-8

*W*hat things about your spouse really bug you? Is it the dirty socks that somehow sneak under your bed? Greasy fingerprints on your best guest towels? His obsession with computer games? His ability to disappear for hours in the hardware store? His selective hearing?

When I think about those little things in my own marriage, I can get bugged—quickly—until I'm humbled by the attitude check in Philippians 2:5-8. For those moments when you're not so sure your mate is heaven-sent (when, frankly, you'd like to send him back to the manufacturer), this next devotional will help.

Did I Take *This* Man?

Two hours before our wedding, Steve, my husband-to-be, was frantically tearing through boxes in our new home, searching for hunting-permit applications he had to turn in that day. "This is important!" Steve said to me over the phone.

I was at the church, my wedding dress half over my head. As my mother held the phone to my ear through all the layers of lace and organza, I reminded him that the photographer was taking pictures before the ceremony.

"I'll be there," he promised. "Just tell me where you put my box of hunting stuff!"

After that episode, it should have come as no surprise that my beloved and I had different interpretations of the vows we exchanged that day. I took his promise to love only me to mean exactly that. Steve, however, thought the promise referred only to forsaking other women—not hunting.

Early in our marriage, I resented the lack of balance in how we spent our time together. If I compared all the time I spent hunting with Steve with the time he spent doing what I love, there'd be no contest. But then I read Philippians 2:5-8: "Your attitude should be the same that Christ Jesus had. Though he was God, he did not demand and cling to his rights as God. He made himself nothing; he took the humble position of a slave and appeared in human form. And in human form he obediently humbled himself even further by dying a criminal's death on a cross."

Such Scripture helped me focus on the many ways Steve loves and helps me rather than on what he's not doing (or I'm doing more of): willingly doing the dishes, believing in my ability as a writer, surprising me with an occasional candlelit dinner for two.

Twenty-three years later, I still love Steve, and he still loves me—despite our first disastrous hunting trip when he forgot the tent poles and matches, and I scared his trophy elk away by screaming when it got too close. There are still times (particularly during hunting season) when I ask myself, *Why did I take this man?* Yet I know that without Steve I'd miss the unique blessings that are the rewards of staying committed.

If you and your spouse are to grow in faith, love, and compassion, it's important to make good choices during all times—whether joyful or difficult.

EILEEN SILVA KINDIG

Recently, Steve and I reminisced our way through a stack of photo albums. As he eagerly turned the pages, I thought, *There's no other person in this entire world who would share the same pleasure in these memories as I do.* My heart swelled with a new level of love for Steve.

I've discovered that time has a way of shrinking differences—and enlarging similarities. And experience has a way of teaching us how to survive the differences that still exist. For instance, Steve is still as passionate about hunting as he was on our wedding day. I'll never derive the same pleasure he does from these outings, but I've learned at least one secret to make them more tolerable: Always pack the tent poles and matches myself. *Mayo Mathers*

A STEP FURTHER

Constants You Can Count On

1. *True love doesn't keep score.* When resentful thoughts creep in, give them to God in prayer.
2. *True love is tolerant.* People you love will respond more readily to you when you try to see things from their perspective before you consider correcting them.
3. *True love believes in the other person.* See possibilities in your spouse. Have faith in your husband, and love him as you work together to achieve God's purposes.
4. *True love requires cultivation.* Remember the importance of the small things—an unexpected gift or an evening at home for just the two of you.
5. *True love hangs in there.* Love remembers the unique blessings that come as a reward of staying committed.   MM

Faith Focus

What do you find annoying about your spouse? How does your response to these annoying habits stack up against Philippians 2:5-8? In what ways can you turn your frustrations with your spouse into exercises in maintaining an eternal perspective, and thereby lower your frustration level?

Prayer Pointer

Thank God for giving you the opportunity to serve your husband. Ask the Lord to make you humble in all you do. Ask him to give you the right words to help your husband lovingly change behaviors he needs to—and the wisdom to know when godly silence is the best response.

LOVE IS PATIENT AND KIND. LOVE
IS NOT JEALOUS OR BOASTFUL OR
PROUD OR RUDE. LOVE DOES NOT
DEMAND ITS OWN WAY. LOVE IS
NOT IRRITABLE, AND IT KEEPS NO
RECORD OF WHEN IT HAS BEEN
WRONGED.

1 CORINTHIANS 13:4-5

*T*wo months after Annie and Rich's wedding, they knew their marriage was in trouble. Both lonely people, they'd assumed their "lonely spots" would be filled by each other. Finally a wise counselor helped them realize they couldn't meet all of each other's needs. "We had to stop keeping track of each other's mistakes," Annie admits, "and learn how to forgive."

To those who have "a little black book" on their spouse, 1 Corinthians responds, "Love . . . keeps no record of when it has been wronged." If you keep track of your spouse's mistakes, here's how—and why—you need to tear up your book.

Do You Have a Little Black Book?

Our pastor told the story of a couple who came to him for counseling. They were active in the church and—as far as everyone knew—happily married. Yet the wife wanted to leave her husband. She said she could no longer take the "black book."

"Show him," the wife said. Her husband reached into his pocket, pulled out a small black notebook, and handed it to the pastor. It didn't take long to see why she was so upset. Her husband had made a list of everything she had done wrong during their marriage!

When I heard that story, I became angry. How could a husband do such a thing? Then it dawned on me. I was as guilty as the man in the story. Maybe I hadn't literally written my husband's wrongs in a little black book, but what I had done was equally damaging. Each time my husband put his job before me, forgot it was Valentine's Day, or let me cry myself to sleep, I wrote down the offense in indelible ink on the pages of my mind.

Soon that "list" became a weapon to haul out during an argument. I was sure that by enumerating each time he'd wronged me, he'd realize what he was doing and change. But I only put him on the defensive. Our arguments became shouting matches. Things became so bad that my husband didn't want to come home at night.

For three years, I begged God to heal my marriage, but things just seemed to get worse. Then my sister offered to pay our way to a weekend marriage retreat and to baby-sit our two toddlers.

During that weekend, I was confronted with the truth: If

I wanted healing in my marriage, I needed to tear up my list. I didn't think I could—I'd been hurt too many times. But through the retreat speaker, God showed me my unforgiving, aching, bitter heart. So when my husband asked, "Will you forgive me?" I made the hardest decision of my life. I stepped out on faith and said, "Yes."

That day I was set free. I wish I could say we lived happily ever after, but that wouldn't be true. The issues we'd argued over for years were still there. But we were freed from the past so we could talk about them without getting defensive. And as our relationship improved, my husband began to open up about things from his past. These insights helped me understand why he was the way he was and moved me toward accepting him, flaws and all.

> *Forgiveness usually isn't a onetime experience. It's an ongoing process. You have to work at it. But the rewards are glorious.*
>
> ELISA MORGAN

If you're keeping even a small list, take time *now* to do something about it. If you don't think you can eliminate the destructive habit of list-keeping on your own, then seek out a pastor or a good Christian counselor to help you.

Recently, my husband told me that at the end of each day, he looks forward to coming home to me. I can't imagine a better compliment. *Judy Bodmer*

A STEP FURTHER

Dos and Don'ts for List Makers!

1. *Do tear up your list.* Advice columnist Ann Landers once wrote, "Forgiveness is setting the prisoner free and then discovering you were the prisoner."

2. *Don't start a new list.* Ephesians 4:26-27 tells us not to let the sun go down on our anger. If we do, the unresolved conflict allows the devil "a mighty foothold." So discuss your conflict instead of remaining quiet and letting it fester.

3. *Don't try to change your husband.* That's God's job.

4. *Do begin a new way of thinking.* Seek out the good in your husband (Phil. 4:8), and tell him what he's doing right.

5. *Do stay alert.* When you feel like starting a new list, lovingly explain your feelings to your husband. Then ask, "Can we make this a new beginning instead?" *JB*

Faith Focus

Do you keep a little black book of your husband's mistakes? If so, what's in it? In order to tear up that book and give your husband a fresh chance, what do you need to do? To forgive and let go of old grudges and hurts? To look instead toward the future with an open mind and heart?

Prayer Pointer

Thank God that he forgave your sins through Christ's death on the cross. Ask him to help you be obedient to Scripture by also forgiving your husband for the ways he's hurt or slighted you. Then pray, asking the Lord to help you move on when you're in looking-back mode.

I PRAY THAT YOUR LOVE FOR EACH
OTHER WILL OVERFLOW MORE AND
MORE, AND THAT YOU WILL KEEP
ON GROWING IN YOUR KNOWL-
EDGE AND UNDERSTANDING.

PHILIPPIANS 1:9

$\mathcal{R}$ick never shares how he feels," my friend Cindy confided in me one day over lunch. "I long to hear how his day went, what he's dreaming about—but when I ask, I get a blank stare."

Have you ever felt that way? If so, you're not alone. I haven't found one wife yet who hasn't felt tuned out of her husband's emotions sometime in her marriage. In fact, another friend admitted, "I think my husband only has three emotions: sleepy, cranky, and hungry!"

So how can we get to know our seemingly emotionless male better? Here's what one man said.

Men Have Emotions Too

"Is something bothering you?" my wife, Elaine, asked as I absentmindedly channel surfed.

"Nope," I replied as I continued to click the TV remote.

"Are you sure? You look kind of down," she persisted.

"Nothing's bothering me. OK?!"

"OK."

Wait a minute! My wife left out something. She's supposed to say, "OK, but if something's bothering you, I'll be glad to listen." And then I'm supposed to answer, "Well . . . (dramatic pause), there's this one thing. . . ."

At least that's how the scene was played from kindergarten to community college in the Charis family. I would be upset; my mother would persist in her questioning; finally I would tell her what was wrong. Unfortunately, I carried that well-worn script into my marriage. And so, many times in Elaine's and my early years together, I never expressed what I was really thinking.

Deep inside, I wanted to tell my wife what kind of day I really had at the office, what I felt when she seemed unsatisfied during our lovemaking, and what I feared about turning forty. But often such sharing was cut short with my quick "Nothing's bothering me."

Although we men don't always express the way we feel, don't be fooled—we still want our wife to know what's going on inside us. You see, for most of our life, we've been told, "Big boys don't cry," and, "Be a man" (meaning, "Don't show emotions"). And so, even though we sometimes feel like crying, we inflict an emotional lobotomy on ourselves. Instead of shedding tears, we secrete stomach acid.

We forget too easily that Jesus provides a positive model of a man who is both tough and tender. He grabs a whip and clears out the dishonest temple merchants, yet sheds tears of grief with his female friends at the tomb of Lazarus.

All of us—man or woman—need a safe haven to express our hopes and fears, moments of pride and humiliation, loves and loathings. And we men need you to know that sometimes we're not only scared but scarred. Each of us carries into marriage wounds such as physical or emotional abuse or feelings of failure over not living up to others' expectations. But because we've played the role of the tough guy who never cries, it's often difficult to let you know those scars.

For husbands and wives who have dual careers, hectic schedules, extensive travel, and different ministries, fostering a closeness of the heart— sharing feelings—is essential..

GAIL C. BENNETT

For instance, it took my friend Bob five years to tell his wife about his abusive childhood. He was afraid she'd think he'd abuse their children. But once it was out, Bob sensed relief and freedom to express years of pent-up feelings.

I continue to be amazed—and maybe a bit envious—that two women can meet as total strangers and within five minutes be discussing their feelings. Somehow, we guys don't often get past, "What do you do for a living?" So be patient with us. And keep gently responding to our "Nothing's bothering me" line with "OK, but if something's bothering you, I'll be glad to listen." Then wait for the dramatic pause.

James Charis

A STEP FURTHER

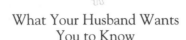

What Your Husband Wants You to Know

1. *I want to please you sexually.* It's humiliating for men to ask for directions, so help us by giving us a road map for sex.
2. *I need you, but I need others, too.* When guys want to know what to *do*, not how to feel, they turn to male friends.
3. *I want to find meaning in my work.* We derive satisfaction from what we do. So support us as we sort out our goals and gifts.
4. *I want to be reconciled with those I love.* Contrary to the "take no prisoners" attitude men express, we're still bothered by unresolved conflict. You can help by asking questions.
5. *I want to remain young and virile forever.* Love us, make us feel we're still sexually desirable, cook us healthy meals, and suggest an aerobic walk around the block.

JC

Faith Focus

How often does your husband open up to you about his feelings, his plans, his dreams? In what ways can you encourage his expression—and also give him the room he needs to think, feel, plan, and dream by himself?

Prayer Pointer

Pray that "your love for each other will overflow more and more, and that you will keep on growing in your knowledge and understanding" (Phil. 1:9) of your spouse.

My goal is that they will be encouraged and knit together by strong ties of love. I want them to have full confidence because they have complete understanding of God's secret plan, which is Christ himself. In him lie hidden all the treasures of wisdom and knowledge.

Colossians 2:2-3

$\mathcal{W}$e never talk."
- "I don't know what he's thinking."
- "We might as well live in different houses, for all we see of each other!"
- "Trying to communicate with him is like talking to a rock."

Have you ever said—or thought—these things in your marriage? Many couples become emotionally distant from each other, at least at some time in their marriage.

But Scripture gives married couples a goal: to be "knit together by strong ties of love" (Col. 2:2). You can become true, intimate partners. Here's how.

Are You and Your Husband Emotionally Miles Apart?

Sally sits at the breakfast table sipping her orange juice while her husband, John, eats his eggs in silence. When he finishes, he leaves with a perfunctory, "See you tonight." Sally doesn't move. She hasn't moved to kiss John and tell him good-bye in years. The sad thing is, he never seems to notice. Every day is the same: John goes his way; Sally goes hers. Sally and John are married—but they are emotionally divorced.

Emotional divorce is a chronic affliction in millions of marriages today. A husband and wife may live under the same roof, share the same bed, parent the same children, and even share the same faith, but they often end up strangers occupying two different worlds emotionally.

The tragedy of emotional divorce is that it doesn't discriminate. It can happen to any couple. Sometimes stressful situations such as unemployment or spiritual incompatibility can cause a rift between husband and wife. But more often than not, it's the little relationship stressors—demanding jobs, too little time together, child-rearing pressures—that erode a couple's emotional intimacy.

The best cure for emotional divorce is prevention. Recognizing danger signals early in your marriage is essential. Withdrawal, arguments over trivial matters, lack of mutual involvement in everyday affairs, and a general feeling of alienation are all important warning signs.

If you want to prevent emotional divorce from occurring in your marriage (or improve intimacy if it's currently nonexistent in your relationship), here are some ideas:

Take time to nurture your relationship. Make it a priority to find out what's happening in your lives without the distractions or interruptions that so easily steal your attention. So build into your lifestyle time for each other. Whether you linger at the dinner table over a cup of coffee after everyone else has eaten or take a quiet walk around the neighborhood when the kids are down for the night, that time together is an investment that pays high dividends in maintaining emotional intimacy.

Love needs to be nurtured.
JAN STOOP

Don't expect your spouse to have the same level of longing for intimacy. Kay's husband, Martin, is a good man who works hard and cares for his family. But he just doesn't seem to require or be comfortable with the kind of sharing and communication Kay craves. A few years ago, she asked herself, *What more can I do to improve the climate of my relationship with my emotionally detached husband?*

Kay finally decided that the more she pushed for emotional intimacy, the more walls Martin put up. So she learned to accept things as they were and find fulfillment in other areas of her life, including trusting God with her emotional needs. She chose to serve her spouse, showing kindness, joy, patience, and love, instead of becoming bitter, defensive, and vengeful.

No matter what emotional state your marriage is in today, hope remains. You can be content as you allow the Lord to heal your heart and work in the heart of your mate according to his wisdom and will. *Jan Silvious*

A STEP FURTHER

Increasing Your Intimacy

1. *Get to know your mate.* Listen to and understand him. Give him room to communicate in his own way.
2. *Learn his love language.* Notice what brings him joy; then make an effort to "speak" his language.
3. *Tell him your love language.* Don't expect him to automatically be fluent.
4. *Don't manipulate your sexual relationship.* Using sexual encounters to reward your husband's "good behavior" or withdrawing sexually when you're angry or hurt will damage your marriage.
5. *Put the past behind you.* If your husband wrongs you but apologizes, forgive him. If you think of something he could do to make it right, discuss it with him. But if there is nothing, leave it out of your conversation.

JS

Faith Focus

Have you and your husband ever faced a time—past
or present—when you've been emotionally distant from
each other? How did the two of you deal with that period
individually and together? What steps do you need to
take to build intimacy into your marriage?

Prayer Pointer

Ask the Lord to give you wisdom
about when to push and when
not to push for intimacy with
your spouse. Thank God that he
is always near you, encouraging
you, even when you and your
spouse are divided emotionally.
Ask him for creative ideas on in-
creasing the flow of love in your
marriage.

I WILL GIVE YOU A NEW HEART
WITH NEW AND RIGHT DESIRES,
AND I WILL PUT A NEW SPIRIT IN
YOU. I WILL TAKE OUT YOUR
STONY HEART OF SIN AND GIVE
YOU A NEW, OBEDIENT HEART.

EZEKIEL 36:26

I've had an affair." Only those who've suffered a spouse's infidelity know the depth of agony those words cause. Such words tear apart the trust and intimacy of a marriage, as Janet and Paul* discovered nine years ago. At first, Janet wanted a divorce—she couldn't imagine sleeping beside or opening her heart to Paul ever again after his infidelity.

Then one morning she discovered Ephesians 4 in her daily quiet time and prayed an honest prayer: *God, I don't want to forgive him, but make me willing—and obedient.*

Here's how one woman learned to forgive—and trust again.

*Names have been changed

Surviving a Husband's Affair

When my husband, Phil, confessed to sexual encounters with four other women during our seventeen-year marriage, I felt as though I were suffocating.

As tears coursed down his cheeks, Phil shared how heavy the burden of his adultery had become, yet how afraid he'd been to tell me. When he finished, we embraced, and somehow I mouthed, "Of course I forgive you. I love you." But his words had forever changed our marriage, and I was filled with rage and horror.

To have kept his sin a secret from me would have spiritually crippled Phil. But its disclosure threatened to cripple *me*. Each day I tearfully confessed to God: "I *will* love Phil. I *choose* to forgive him." But at night I'd slip from our bed to weep because of the ugly thoughts that engulfed me.

Our relationship was strained. Arguments erupted without warning. After one particularly volatile fight, I ran to a nearby park to be alone. As I wept, I picked up the Bible I'd instinctively brought along and found Micah 4:9. It was as if God were telling me, "You're behaving as one who has no hope. Always remember you indeed have a king—me." I'd counted on Phil to meet all my needs; now Jesus took his rightful place.

On that day I vowed never again to display despair. I also realized I needed to cancel the debt Phil owed me for his unfaithfulness. When I returned home, I shared with Phil what God had revealed to me, and we forgave each other for the cruel words we'd exchanged.

Meanwhile, Phil also was being tutored through God's Word. Psalm 51 seared into his heart, becoming his own sincere plea before the Lord. He grieved to see not only how he'd devastated me by his adultery but how he'd sinned against God himself.

Many years later, as our twentieth anniversary approached, we planned to renew our marriage vows in a simple ceremony with only our three children present. As I cheerfully asked Jesus what special gift I could give Phil, he quickly responded, *Give him the gift of a bride's trust.*

I stopped cold. To completely trust again—as though the adulteries had never occurred—would make me vulnerable! But in the days that followed, the Lord showed me I had to release the record of Phil's wrongs I'd stored in my heart.

> *Before you can feel compassion or alleviate discord, you must recognize God's unconditional forgiveness and adopt that same attitude toward your spouse. You must be willing to forgive as you wish to be forgiven.*
> JUDITH LECHMAN

When our anniversary arrived, Phil vowed to be faithful to me and slipped a new diamond ring on my finger. Then I held his hands and announced my own gift to him: the trust of a bride. He was visibly moved, for he knew God had graciously wiped the slate clean not only in heaven but also in my heart.

This May marks our twenty-fifth anniversary. By God's grace and the Holy Spirit's faithfulness, past failures no longer drown out God's gentle voice for our future together in him.

A. M. Swanson

A STEP FURTHER

Mending Your Marriage

1. *Don't handle it alone.* Get professional help from a counselor or pastor for severe crises, such as adultery, in your marriage.
2. *Talk—and listen.* Share hopes, dreams, hurts, and feelings. But let what you do and say be governed by God's love. As you become more aware of each other's past experiences, pray that God will grant you more compassion for each other.
3. *Realize it takes time to rebuild trust.* Don't expect—or push for—overnight changes.
4. *Read the Bible and pray together.* Let God's Word, rather than your words, do the convicting in his heart. A good place to start is Psalm 51.
5. *Recognize that your husband can't meet all your needs.* Let Jesus take his rightful place. AMS

Faith Focus

Have you, or someone you know, suffered a spouse's infidelity? How did hearing the news make you feel? If you've been betrayed, what steps (if any) have you and your spouse taken to mend your relationship in a God-honoring way? Have you forgiven him for the affair—and asked God to help you move on?

Prayer Pointer

If your marriage vows have been put to the test, ask God to give you compassion, discernment, and a forgiving heart. If someone you know has suffered infidelity, pray for both spouses—that they'll be open to hearing God's voice.

Jesus told them, "I assure you, if you have faith and don't doubt, you can do things like this and much more. You can even say to this mountain, 'May God lift you up and throw you into the sea,' and it will happen. If you believe, you will receive whatever you ask for in prayer."

MATTHEW 21:21-22

*I*t was a simple sign, hanging above an elderly couple's bed. But it had a powerful message: "The couple who prays together, stays together." And Luci and Henry have been praying together for more than fifty years!

In an age where many marriages end in divorce, Christian couples would be wise to pay attention to such advice. As Luci and Henry say, "That sign reminds us that nothing's worth going to bed mad over. So we pray until the 'mads' go away!"

Here's how you and your spouse can become prayer warriors.

Prayer Warriors

I was only seven, but I remember that morning vividly. After throwing off my bedcovers, I padded down the hallway toward the kitchen of our Colorado home in my pajamas. But in the doorway, I stopped. In childlike awe, I watched my parents as they sat at the kitchen table, hands clasped together and heads bowed in prayer as they talked to God about whether my father should take a new college and seminary teaching position in another country or continue their current ministry.

And that wasn't the first or the only time I'd seen my parents pray together. They've prayed about and during all our moves—from the east coast to the midwest, to the northwest, to Canada, then back to the midwest. They thanked God in all times—in plenty and in want, when needed income didn't come in.

They also prayed for my older sister, Evangeline, and for me—for our physical, emotional, and, most of all, spiritual health. They prayed when I stepped on a rusty nail on my grandparents' Iowa farm and had to be rushed to the doctor; when my sister had to have foot surgery; when I got tonsillitis and then pneumonia in high school.

And now that my sister and I are "all grown up," my parents still pray for us—and for our additions to the family! Although we're currently states apart, we talk on the phone each Saturday morning, sharing our hopes, happenings, thanksgivings, and prayer requests.

Watching my parents' "pray-about-everything" attitude has affected my life to its very core. I've seen, with my own eyes, that prayer *does* have the power to change a situation. One afternoon, when my father hadn't been paid for his ministry work once again and my mother knew we had little food left, she got on her knees in the kitchen and prayed. Several hours later, a car pulled up—loaded with all sorts of wonderful groceries!

It's no wonder, then, after seeing the power of prayer as a child, that I approached marriage with my husband, Jeff, in the same light.

> *If your plans as a couple are to have value and potential, then God must be involved in that planning through prayer.*
> JUDY DOUGLASS

Since we were youth leaders at a local church, we became instant "surrogate parents" two days after our honeymoon to an active bunch of junior high and high schoolers: celebrating their joys, listening to their sorrows and questions about Christianity, sex, relationships, family. It was an awful lot to do! Kneeling down before our first "couple" Bible study with the kids, we prayed, "Lord, we feel overwhelmed. Give us patience and wisdom to help them become God-honoring adults!"

Today, twelve years later, we praise God for all the ways he's honored that request (and numerous others along the way!). Just yesterday, when one of "our kids" phoned from her overseas ministry to say, "Thanks for being my prayer warriors all these years," I cried. How glad Jeff and I are that God is now using us, as he's used my parents in our lives, to pray together for the advancement of his kingdom!

Ramona Cramer Tucker

A STEP FURTHER

Becoming Prayer Partners

1. *Set aside time*. Yes, pray at meals, but also set aside a fifteen-minute time slot when you can pray together without being interrupted. Soon you'll long for more.
2. *Pray honestly*. Don't use prayer as a way of pointing out how your spouse should change. Instead, pray that you'll change; then let God work on your spouse.
3. *Pray by category*. For instance, if you have "couple prayer time" each Saturday morning, pray for your relationship on the first Saturday, your children and/or extended family on the second Saturday, your church/missionaries on the third, and your community/the world on the fourth.
4. *Read a book about prayer*. Or pray through the Scriptures. This activity will increase the intimacy of your relationship with God—and each other.   *RCT*

Faith Focus

How often do you and your spouse pray together (other than the traditional praying over food)? What steps could you take to set aside a special time regularly for this important event?

Prayer Pointer

Thank God that he's always ready to listen, that you can be confident he'll always hear your prayers (1 John 5:14-15). Ask the Lord to hold you accountable to him and to each other to pray together regularly.

LOVE EACH OTHER WITH GENUINE
AFFECTION, AND TAKE DELIGHT IN
HONORING EACH OTHER.

ROMANS 12:10

$\mathcal{I}$f you asked your husband, "How can I show you I love you?" what do you think he'd say?

Being a curious woman, I asked my husband. "Give me a back rub," Jeff said, grinning. "Make me mashed potatoes and gravy. Let me relax for a few minutes after work before we have to go anywhere. And hug me whenever I walk in the door." Interestingly enough, none of those gifts costs money. How true Romans 12:10 is: Each of us longs to be loved "with *genuine* affection" and "delight"!

Want *your* husband to feel special? Try these tips.

Gifts You Can Give Your Marriage

It was the day before my birthday, and my husband, Jack, had to get to the airport to catch an early morning flight. As I got up, dressed hastily, and dropped Jack off at the terminal, I couldn't help feeling sad that he was going to be out of town for my birthday.

But when I returned home and went upstairs to finish my morning routine, I noticed scrawled on the bathroom mirror in eyebrow pencil a handwritten note that read, "Happy Birthday! I Love You."

A note of joy sounded in my heart. As I found other notes throughout my day—under the soap dish; on the shower door, the TV screen, kitchen counter, microwave oven—with the same message, that first joyful note in my heart grew into a full-blown symphony that drowned out my loneliness.

The gift Jack gave me that morning was far more precious than the wrapped present and card he'd left behind—and it didn't cost him anything except time, thought, creativity, and sacrifice.

Here are several gifts filled with thoughtfulness and wrapped in love that you can give your spouse anytime:

The gift of changed behavior. What change would make your husband feel valued? The gift of punctuality or no nagging? "Change is the name of the game," says an old adage. That's especially true in marriage. Our willingness to change is one of the greatest gifts we can give our spouse.

The gift of companionship. Ask your husband to list the top ten things that add to his enjoyment of life. Then determine to add one of his choices to your life by reading a book about it, taking lessons, or participating with him (even if it's just watching his tennis game every Monday).

The gift of initiating. In his book *Letters to Karen,* well-known author Charlie Shedd makes a powerful statement: "It matters everything to a man if he has a home where he knows he is of inestimable value." So plan date nights, come up with vacation ideas, take the initiative in lovemaking.

The gift of time with friends. Is there an old friend your husband hasn't seen for a while? Invite him over for dinner; then vacate the dining room after supper so they can talk. Or buy your husband two tickets to a sporting event and suggest he take a friend.

The gift of "buffer" time. Offer your husband fifteen to thirty minutes of quiet after work before you suggest he play with the children or communicate with you.

Little acts of thoughtfulness go a long way toward building healthy relationships and making someone feel comfortable.

CLAUDIA ARP

The gift of prayer. Spend ten minutes a day for one month praying just for your husband. Ask God to give you wisdom and ideas, and soon those ten minutes will be too short!

Love and marriage take work—there's no getting around it. But the price you pay in thought, time, and caring when you give "I love you" gifts shows those you love that you treasure them.   *Carole Mayhall*

A Step Further

Zesty Gift Idea

1. *Create a "love basket."* Write fifty-two things you know your husband would love to do or have done (such as have a taco party with his buddies, get a back rub, have someone clean the garage) on slips of paper. Have your husband choose one slip each week for a year.
2. *Take on one of his chores for a day or a week.*
3. *Encourage his hobbies.* If he wants to learn more about car repair, borrow a book from the library or sign him up for that dream class at a local college.
4. *Serve him breakfast in bed.* This little extra—especially on a more relaxed Saturday morning—can restore the twinkle in love's eye.

CM

Faith Focus

What gifts does your husband respond to? What gift could you give him this week to put zest into your relationship and a smile on his face?

Prayer Pointer

Pray for your husband—and for the many roles he plays at home, work, and church. Ask God to reveal to you ways in which you could surprise your husband. Ask the Lord to help you to be thoughtful and loving in your responses to your husband.

LET YOUR WIFE BE A FOUNTAIN
OF BLESSING FOR YOU. REJOICE IN
THE WIFE OF YOUR YOUTH. SHE IS
A LOVING DOE, A GRACEFUL DEER.
LET HER BREASTS SATISFY YOU AL-
WAYS. MAY YOU ALWAYS BE CAP-
TIVATED BY HER LOVE.

PROVERBS 5:18-19

*G*ladys and Glenn have been married for sixty years. "The first twenty were miserable," Glenn says. "But the last forty—I wouldn't trade 'em for anything!" Because these Montana old-timers have a passion for helping others develop healthy marriages, they hold a two-hour seminar in their barn each Saturday night. "We want to encourage young folks to love and respect each other and to put God first."

Because of Gladys and Glenn, hundreds of couples are now "captivated by [each other's] love." If you, too, want a happy marriage, here's what you should know.

Eight Secrets to a Happy Marriage

What keeps a marriage happy throughout the years? How do couples survive the tough times—and manage to keep their marriage alive and growing? Here's an inside look at the eight key ingredients to keeping your marriage happy.

Use the right "super glue." Happy couples share a commitment to God. When a wife can share the deepest things of her heart with her husband, there is true contentment and lasting joy. When other factors in a marriage are weak, this one—a mutual love for God and desire to serve him—can keep two people determined to work toward a relationship that reflects God's love and power.

Be friends as well as lovers. Most women rate "love and affection" number one when they list what they desire most from marriage. Most men rate "companionship" at the top—even above sex. Doing things together—reading quietly, driving in friendly silence, sharing a joke, or playing tennis together—is vital. Happy couples play together, enjoy what the other enjoys, and laugh together.

Tune in to pillow talk. Happy couples make the time and effort to explore each other's soul: to openly share joys, successes, hurts, dreams, and fears without rejection. But for that kind of communication to exist, each partner must understand and accept the other's differences.

Refuse to win. One gauge of marital happiness is how effectively couples deal with anger, conflict, and frustration. When one spouse sets out to "win," both spouses lose. Happy couples solve their conflicts so they both win—with a mutually satisfying resolution.

Happy couples work through the majors, shrug off the

minors, and are mature enough to know the difference.

Stay true-blue. Happy couples are faithful. Fidelity was a given for the one hundred couples Dr. Catherine Johnson, author of *Lucky in Love*, interviewed about the secret to their happiness: "For them, being faithful to each other was not what made a marriage happy—it was what made a marriage possible in the first place."

Make room for change. Happy couples realize that in marriage, "change is the name of the game." They see the truth in Proverbs 27:17, realizing that when two lives rub together daily, sparks can fly. But as changes occur, each person becomes more Christlike.

The key principle of our marriage is: If God's first, everything else falls in line. Because Alvin loves God, I don't have to worry about him loving me.
CECE WINANS

Keep the flame burning. Happy couples know the value of time and romance. Sex is part of romance, but touching, holding hands, meeting eyes across a room, winking or smiling over a family joke are also part of it.

Act as one flesh. Happy couples realize that marriage is a team sport, not a competition. Each carries the other when he or she is down. Happy couples don't lead separate lives; they refer to "our money" and "our plans." They have grasped the significance of 1 Peter 3:8: "Finally, all of you should be of one mind, full of sympathy toward each other, loving one another with tender hearts and humble minds."   *Carole Mayhall*

A Step Further

Tips for Marital Bliss

1. *Be president of each other's fan club.*
   Cheerlead for your spouse (1 Cor. 13:7)
   at his favorite activity.
2. *Work on true intimacy.* Strive for a deeper
   level of communication. Accept and
   respect each other's differences.
3. *Keep a short account.* Forgive—and don't
   hold grudges. Bringing up past differences
   separates spouses in the present and future.
4. *Budget time and money for a marriage
   retreat every year.* And don't forget the
   importance of date nights—try for one
   night at least every other week!
5. *Love each other—unconditionally.* That's
   the way God loves you. Doesn't your
   spouse deserve the same treatment?
6. *Pray together, if your spouse is a Christian.*
   Ask God to make your union strong—
   and give him the credit.   CM

Faith Focus

On a scale of one (we could use help—fast!) to ten (we have a great marriage), where would you rate yours?

Which of the eight secrets to success could you and your spouse use to work toward a healthier, happier marriage?

Prayer Pointer

Thank God for the gift of your marriage. Ask the Lord to bring to mind the tools you can use to make your marriage happier and healthier. Thank him in advance for the ways in which you and your spouse can grow together— spiritually, emotionally, mentally, and physically!

"AT LAST!" ADAM EXCLAIMED. "SHE IS PART OF MY OWN FLESH AND BONE! SHE WILL BE CALLED 'WOMAN,' BECAUSE SHE WAS TAKEN OUT OF A MAN." THIS EXPLAINS WHY A MAN LEAVES HIS FATHER AND MOTHER AND IS JOINED TO HIS WIFE, AND THE TWO ARE UNITED INTO ONE.

GENESIS 2:23-24

*J*ust imagine what it was like to be the first man and woman on earth: the wonder of seeing someone who looked like you yet was different; the delight of finally having a companion created especially for you!

Scripture says that when a couple joins in marriage, "the two are united into one." But how exactly can two people—with varying backgrounds, personalities, talents—agree on a common, unified purpose?

If you long to become more of a "single unit" but it seems impossible at times, here's how to turn that longing into a "mission possible"—with God's help.

Mission Possible

"You have a *what?*" my friend Jana asked me.

"A mission statement for our marriage," I said again, as we sipped iced tea at a local restaurant. "Before Jeff and I got engaged, we wanted to make sure we'd be doing something together for God that otherwise we wouldn't have done on our own, as singles."

"You're so weird," Jana said half-laughing, half-serious. "What difference does that make—either way you're serving God, right?"

"Well, both of us were happy as singles and busily involved with our church. We felt strongly that God wanted us to marry, but we wanted to maintain our ministry focus," I explained. "So we drafted a mission statement for our marriage to keep us on target."

Now, twelve years into our marriage, we're glad we did. As friends have gotten married (and some divorced), we've seen some couples disappear into "La-la Land"—only to emerge a year later, discovering they've lost all their other friends. Others pursue separate hobbies more than "spouse" time. There are precious few who balance time with each other; time alone to develop individual interests; time with friends, family, and church; and time with God.

If you and your spouse were to sit down today to write a mission statement for your marriage, what would you say? What do you and your spouse want to accomplish together? What could you do now that you wouldn't have been able to accomplish as a single?

Our friends Becky and Mike are great at hospitality. On her own, Becky's almost timid—but she's a good listener and a great cook. On his own, Mike could overwhelm his guests with his jovial nature. But together they make a warm, powerful team that's drawn many toward God.

My single friend Star longed to be a missionary to a Muslim country, but no missionary board would accept her (single women are not respected in Arab culture). Then she met Jon, who shared her passion for missions. They've been ministering to the Arab world now for six years.

> *Marriage is a journey, not a destination. It's a marathon, not a sprint. It's a lifetime union of two imperfect people who love each other.*
> CLAUDIA ARP

As for Jeff and me, our teamwork has helped me slow down and gain perspective. Although we're both on-the-go personalities, Jeff is good at knowing when to rest. I could, like the Energizer Bunny, keep going until my batteries completely run out and I spend a week in bed, sick. Together we're learning to balance our drive to not only accomplish our own work but also be Christlike role models.

What's our mission statement?
- To love each other faithfully and forgive unconditionally, as God loves and forgives us
- To help each other grow mentally, emotionally, and spiritually
- To reach out to others in hospitality, sacrificial friendship, and with the good news of Jesus

These few words are enough to keep a marriage on the right track—and more than enough to do to last a lifetime!

Ramona Cramer Tucker

A STEP FURTHER

Enhancing Your Partnership

1. *Set aside an evening just for you.* Go to a quiet restaurant, or spend the night at a hotel. Focus on your future together and the desires you'd like to see fulfilled.

2. *Answer these questions together:*
   - What do I love best about this marriage?
   - If I could change one thing about this marriage, what would it be?
   - How can we help each other grow?
   - How can we reach out more to others?
   - Are we advancing the cause of Christ?

3. *Draft three statements about what you most want from your life together.* The following subpoints will get you started:

   Our Marriage:
   Others:
   God:

4. *Post your Marriage Mission Statement in a prominent place as a daily reminder.*

RCT

Faith Focus

In what ways do you and your spouse balance each other—make each other a better person? Do you know what you want from your marriage? If you and your spouse don't yet have a mission statement for your marriage, why not set aside some time over the next month to draft one?

Prayer Pointer

Thank God for the wonderful gift of your spouse (even when you don't feel very thankful!). Ask God to open your and your spouse's eyes to appreciate even more what you can do *together!*

ACKNOWLEDGMENTS

Today's Christian Woman magazine and Tyndale House Publishers would like to thank TCW staff members Barbara Calvert, Joy McAuley, and Jane Johnson Struck for their help in the editorial/permission process, and the following people who graciously gave their permission to adapt the following material from *Today's Christian Woman* in this book.

Arp, Claudia. "Is Your Spouse Driving You Nuts?" (March/April 1995).

Bodmer, Judy. "My Little Black Book" (September/October 1993).

Brooks, C. C. *One Woman's Story*, "I Had to Fall in Love with My Husband . . . Again" (January/February 1995).

Charis, James. "What Your Husband Wants You to Know" (July/August 1995); "Can We Talk?" (March/April 1996). http://members.tripod.com/~jimcharis

Harris, Janis Long. "Four of a Kind" (July/August 1990); "Who's Minding the Money?" (September/October 1995).

Higgs, Liz Curtis. "Married . . . with Antlers" (July/August 1995).

Mathers, Mayo. "Did I Take *This* Man?" (September/October 1996).

Mayhall, Carole. "Get Closer" (January/February 1991); "The Stale Mate" (May/June 1991); "How Does Your Marriage Sound . . . When You Think No One Is Listening?" (May/June 1992); "Great Expectations" (July/August 1992); "Happily Married . . .

What's the Secret?" (January/February 1993); "Gifts You Can Give Your Marriage" (November/December 1993).

Moser, Nancy. "Reconcilable Differences" (November/December 1996).

Newenhuyse, Elizabeth Cody. "Why Can't He Be More Like . . . " (July/August 1990); "Moving Is the Pits" (November/December 1991); "Is Your Husband a 'Lone Ranger'?" (March/April 1997).

Oeth, Annie. *One Woman's Story*, "Faith in the Face of Recession" (July/August 1992).

Schimmels, Cliff. "What I Didn't Know about 'I Do' before I Did" (July/August 1996).

Silvious, Jan. "Another Kind of Divorce" (March/April 1992).

Smith, Harold B. "If Fitting Rooms Could Talk" (March/April 1990).

Stiles, LaNelle C. "Married to Mr. Clean" (May/June 1993).

Strobel, Lee. "We Were Spiritually Mismatched" (May/June 1993).

Swanson, A. M. *One Woman's Story*, "Could Our Marriage Survive My Husband's Affairs?" (March/April 1992).